The Darkest Night Brings Longer Days

Footprints Series
Jane Errington, Editor

The life stories of individual women and men who were participants in interesting events help nuance larger historical narratives, at times reinforcing those narratives, at other times contradicting them. The Footprints series introduces extraordinary Canadians, past and present, who have led fascinating and important lives at home and throughout the world.

The series includes primarily original manuscripts but may consider the English-language translation of works that have already appeared in another language. The editor of the series welcomes inquiries from authors. If you are in the process of completing a manuscript that you think might fit into the series, please contact her, care of McGill-Queen's University Press, 1010 Sherbrooke Street West, Suite 1720, Montreal, QC, H3A 2R7.

The Darkest Night Brings Longer Days

Surviving War and Iran's Evin Prison

SIROUS HOUSHMAND

McGill-Queen's University Press
Montreal & Kingston • London • Chicago

ISBN 978-0-2280-2577-1 (paper)
ISBN 978-0-2280-2578-8 (ePDF)
ISBN 978-0-2280-2579-5 (ePUB)

Legal deposit third quarter 2025
Bibliothèque et Archives nationales du Québec

Printed in Canada on acid-free paper that is 100% ancient-forest-free, containing 100% sustainable, recycled fibre, and processed chlorine-free.

Funded by the Government of Canada | Financé par le gouvernement du Canada | Canada | Canada Council for the Arts | Conseil des arts du Canada

We acknowledge the support of the Canada Council for the Arts.
Nous remercions le Conseil des arts du Canada de son soutien.

McGill-Queen's University Press in Montreal is on land which long served as a site of meeting and exchange amongst Indigenous Peoples, including the Haudenosaunee and Anishinabeg nations. In Kingston it is situated on the territory of the Haudenosaunee and Anishinaabek. We acknowledge and thank the diverse Indigenous Peoples whose footsteps have marked these territories on which peoples of the world now gather.

Library and Archives Canada Cataloguing in Publication

Title: The darkest night brings longer days : surviving war and Iran's Evin Prison / Sirous Houshmand.
Names: Houshmand, Sirous, author.
Series: Footprints series (Montréal, Quebec) ; 31.
Description: Series statement: Footprints series ; 31 | Includes bibliographical references and index.
Identifiers: Canadiana (print) 20250178117 | Canadiana (ebook) 2025017815X | ISBN 9780228025771 (paper) | ISBN 9780228025795 (ePUB) | ISBN 9780228025788 (ePDF)
Subjects: LCSH: Houshmand, Sirous—Imprisonment. | LCSH: Ivīn (Prison) | LCSH: Political prisoners—Iran—Biography. | LCGFT: Autobiographies.
Classification: LCC DS318.84.H68 A3 2025 | DDC 365/.48092—dc23

This book was designed and typeset by studio oneonone in Minion 12/15.
Copyediting by Eleanor Gasparik.

McGill-Queen's University Press
Suite 1720, 1010 Sherbrooke St West, Montreal, QC, H3A 2R7

Authorized safety representative in the EU: Mare Nostrum Group BV, Mauritskade 21D, 1091 GC Amsterdam, the Netherlands, gpsr@mare-nostrum.co.uk

I dedicate this book to Khosrow, Naser, Jahangir, and the thousands of others who perished in Evin Prison during the 1988 mass executions. They believed in people's capacity to harness their intrinsic greed and forge equitable relationships, knowing that, as Alain Badiou observed, "Love without risk is an impossibility, like war without death." They passionately lived, loved, and died in search of a different world.

Perhaps, one day, the sun will rise over
a different world after all.

Contents

Figures

The
Darkest Night
Brings
Longer Days

Prologue

It's not easy to imagine yourself held captive in Iran's Evin Prison, having no idea when they will release you or take your life.

Most people won't experience such extreme circumstances as political imprisonment. But being in the depths of isolation reveals nuanced human behaviour that might surprise you. Can you hold on to your dearest values, survive by paying an undesirable price, or yield to something in between? Is it more honourable to stand up to bullying or more convenient to remain on the sidelines? How far can you be pushed before you say no?

Tehran's notorious Evin Prison was built in 1971 during the regime of Mohammad Reza Pahlavi, or the Shah. Its purpose was to create space for an increasing number of political prisoners. Originally, the prison had a capacity for 320 inmates; in 1977, it expanded to accommodate 1,500 prisoners; in 1983, the population had ballooned to approximately 15,000 inmates.[1] SAVAK – the Organization of National Security and

Information – operated these facilities during the Shah's regime, where numerous political prisoners were held in terrifying conditions, tortured, and executed. After the revolution in 1979, the Islamic Republic of Iran's judiciary branch managed the prison. According to many observers, during this time, Evin's reputation for inhumane conditions, torture, and execution didn't change and, at certain times, became horrifyingly intolerable.

Years before his captivity, a twelve-year-old Iranian boy matures and adapts to his new environment after being thrown into an unfamiliar and seemingly glamorous Western way of life. To compete with his peers in the United States, he must refine his skills and recognize the power of self-determination.

Slowly, the boy becomes a man, aware of the contrast between confidence and ego, realism and fantasy, but still dissatisfied with his life. For him, acquiring material goods, travelling, and forming casual relationships are undeniably pleasurable; however, he finds that joy has a different texture. He begins looking for the more authentic aspects of life, like the delight of looking a loved one in the eye, the thrill of marvelling at an artistic creation, the excitement of loving a person, the fascination of searching for meaning in life, the intrigue of being a rebel, or the exhilaration of fighting for a cause larger than himself. Similarly, as a rookie industrial engineer, he finds his newly acquired status pleasurable, yet the satisfaction derived from comforting people brings him a different sensation. As time passes, he becomes convinced that to experience a more enduring joy, he must change the direction of his life.

That boy, that man, is me.

By appreciating the impact of failure and its transformative qualities, I moved closer to a different level of realization. Such awareness deeply affected how I saw the world, questioned myself, re-examined my priorities, and attuned myself to a new reality.

But with awareness came a critical assessment of the social system's inherent capacity to generate unrestrained socio-economic excesses. While listening to my co-workers, I became more aware of suffering and how those around me were thrown into a world of conformity to make a living wage. Every day, I aimed to find enough courage to question these systemic flaws and discover the audacity to hope for a different world. I realized that joyfully weathering the storm of life would be more desirable than living securely on the shore, simply existing.

Partially because of this quest, I was propelled away from the West and consequently found myself in Iran during the 1979 revolution. Predisposed to feel involved in some capacity, I was intensely swept inside the storm of this momentous period.

In Iran, while acclimating to a home I had left many years earlier – especially dealing with language inadequacies – I found myself, first, a willing follower of the revolution, then a medical aide in the Iran-Iraq War, and, finally, a prisoner of the regime. The authorities swept me up amid a widespread assault against the opposition, and as a secular activist, I was sent to the infamous Evin Prison. I was there during the 1988 mass executions when thousands of fellow political prisoners died. Amid these horrifying days, the conflict between love and survival persistently confronted me. I found that the conviction of the human spirit, regardless of its substance, can spur resistance and passion.

While moving from one prison cell to another, I befriended several exceptional people with transformative qualities. The camaraderie we cultivated became a light in the darkest hours. As our suffering continued, my bond with them grew. One by one, I watched them, along with many others, be taken away.

Not more than a handful came out alive.

After my imprisonment, I found myself grappling with a dilemma: What should I say to friends who might ask about my past? Should I tell them about my time in Evin Prison and the incredibly low odds of my survival?

While attempting to live a "normal life," my past affected my outlook, making me more introspective, politically aware, and less indifferent to the suffering of others. In the early years, I couldn't escape the recurring dreadful thoughts of my time in captivity. They haunted me in both my sleep and waking hours. But in time, I've learned to live with them, even if they occasionally find their way into my dreams.

My father, a significant figure in my childhood, has had a profound influence on how I perceive the world. As a physician, his unwavering empathy toward the underprivileged and his firmness with affluent patients have left an enduring impression on me. By the time I returned to Iran after years of living abroad, he had retired, and I welcomed the opportunity to have many delightful conversations with him.

In 2001, I stepped into a hospital room to bid him a final farewell. It was a moment of unbearable pain and heart-rending sorrow. My eyes, tear-filled, looked into his; his gaze spoke volumes. He knew this was the end of his remarkable life. He was my rock, my guiding light, and my moral compass; his death was a devastating blow from which I had to find a way to recover.

As a young man, the revolutionary fervour of the 1960s in the United States, the Kent State University shootings, the drift of many toward consumerism, the struggle of women and their hopes for liberation, society's pressures to conform, and the establishment's manoeuvres to control were all astonishingly eye-opening. Yet, simultaneously, there were many moments of joy when I felt parachuted into the middle of exciting events I had never experienced before.

Living in two different worlds influenced me during almost unfathomable circumstances. My first world in the United States was calm, quiet, and comfortable. Yet, it made me realize various positive and negative aspects of life, a recognition that would later become transformative. My second world, in Iran, involved intense excitement and, later, an unbearable amount of pain and suffering.

Looking back, in the thick of the most dangerous moments, my perception of war must have been naive. As a medical volunteer, the images of slaughter boggled my mind; it's impossible to put such brutality into words. It was an unparalleled experience finding myself in a siege with all its atrocities, not once but twice. However, the paradox of seeing acts of humanity amid brutality was also transforming.

I met Pegah before my imprisonment, a charming girl. She worked for an agency serving refugees. Within a year of our marriage, we had a baby boy. Pegah, my son, and my parents went through hell during my time in Evin Prison – I don't think anyone, prisoners or their families, is immune from the trauma of such cruelty. Imprisonment reinforced our strong relationship, and it was in good standing for decades until our worlds steadily changed; in time, we agreed to part ways.

Interrogation, prison life, and, eventually, the painful period of the executions compelled me to look inward and re-examine the meaning of life. In particular, I puzzled over the intricacies of human behaviour, especially why some rebel against their social condition and others don't.

My friends who died in prison resisted pressures compelling them to live a normal life and be tranquillized to the suffering of others. On the contrary, they remained uncorrupted. Through my writing, I hope to honour their passing by bringing their aspirations and thoughts to life, inspiring political discourse and challenging possible indifference.

It is here that I begin my story.

Names and identifying details of certain individuals involved have been changed or omitted to protect their privacy.

1
Observing and Discovering

The opposite of an idealist is too often a man without love.
Albert Camus

I was prepared to see the door open and hear one of the prison guards shout, "All your belongings," code for, "You are coming with me to line up for mass execution."

My eyes were fixed on the impenetrable door, knowing its latch would inevitably move to one side.

"I need to focus!" I mumbled to myself. But my mind was racing in many directions. Suddenly, a feeling of numbness came over me. I was weary of stressful thoughts, yet there were moments when I couldn't hold them back.

Glancing at a young political prisoner beside me, I asked, "What do you miss?"

"In these dire moments, my thoughts drift every which way," he said.

"Are you frightened?" I asked.

"Fear seems irrelevant when one feels detached from the present moment," he said. I nodded, feeling the weight of our shared plight and having no desire to reflect on whatever was to happen. It was too distressing.

"Perhaps, when a tragedy is imminent, one isn't eager to grasp its impact," I whispered. "Fear is more pronounced when there is a separation in time between you and what you fear."

Anticipating that the guards would enter any minute, I went on.

"It's remarkable – in our minds, the beauty of life and its vitality diminishes when we dally in 'everydayness.' Yet, when faced with an existential threat, our attention refocuses on its dazzling allure. Death gives meaning to life. Deep thoughts arise from a simple walk through the cemetery. Yet, at the same time, and ironically, we justify our cause for living as grounds for dying. What's more," I continued, "one's destiny can change instantly. After this affair, my son's life will be entirely different."

We both knew that an agonizing ordeal loomed, one that would undeniably chart a different path for our families.

As I tried to fathom the magnitude of my predicament, I recalled when I was nine years old.

Almost every summer weekend around 1960, my father would organize trips to different villages in a city's periphery some kilometres away from Tehran. I felt lucky to be included, especially travelling to the base of Aresk Mountain – part of the Alborz Mountain range – whose majestic peak towered gracefully above others. Our trip's pretext was hunting; however, as the city's primary physician and the health department's managing director, my father would first see all the people in that village who needed medical help. Usually, the people accompanying him included my brothers, his assistant nurse, other friends, and me.

During a visit, a prominent member of the township or village would usually invite us to his house. Quickly, a queue would form with my father seated at the front, his assistant next to him, my older brother third, and my other brother at the end. As the youngest of the siblings, I was typically a spectator.

Due to a lack of a permanent medical facility nearby, most inhabitants were eager to take advantage of the occasion, even if they were free of any medical issues – they didn't know when a doctor would come around again. After the checkup, my father would point to his assistant and explain the situation if a severe case were detected. Then, medicine was administered, or arrangements were made to transport the patient to the city. On the other hand, if the case were not serious, he would point to my older brother, who dispensed certain drugs. Finally, if someone wanted to be examined but was completely healthy and had dreamt up some symptoms, my other brother would be called into action.

"Doctor, I feel weak in the mornings," the person might say.

"Okay, let me examine you." My father would pull out his stethoscope and conduct a thorough examination. "You don't have a serious problem, but let me give you something; it might help." His unique ability to connect with his patients and understand their needs was exceptional. He could detect the ones he knew wouldn't be happy if left untreated.

"Please give this person some of those pills," he would say to my brother at the end of the medical receiving line.

Then, without naming the medication, my brother would dole out a packet of vitamin C and advise on the dosage. Most villagers were pleased with the vitamins and left satisfied.

Typically, we would devote the first day of our trip to the people needing examinations. The second day was set aside for hunting. As a young child, I was greatly affected by the philanthropic aspects of these trips, especially since they were usually taken during my father's leisure time. All medicines were distributed free of charge. More importantly, these services were implemented in a way that upheld the dignity and self-respect of the treated, and we were frequently reminded not to lose sight of this matter. Later in life, and even after my father passed away, many remembered him with affection and admiration when I visited some villages in that region.

I was eleven when my family needed to decide: should we move to the United States for the children's education? After much deliberation, the family decided that my three siblings and mother would go in a few months. I was to stay with my father for one year and complete grade six, after which my father and I would join the others. When they left, I enrolled at an elementary school in the city where my father worked. I relished having one-on-one time with him and have many fond memories.

Once, my father and I arrived at our destination early in the morning, ready to hunt partridges or quails. These birds usually hide under bushes or rocks during the day; by walking randomly around the hillside, one could startle them out of their hiding places, but we had a different plan. We decided to sit in a ditch close to a spring just before sunrise, concealing ourselves behind large boulders. We knew they would come out to feed close to dawn or dusk. It was a strategy I hadn't experienced before, and the anticipation was so intense, it filled the air with excitement.

As we waited for the sun to rise above the mountain's crest, the beauty of the spring and its surroundings was mesmerizing. The fresh, earthy scent of the green vegetation covered large parts of the landscape while the early morning mist had already settled over the foliage. The icy-cold, crystal-clear water from the mountain's depths cascaded into a pond, at the far end of which the same pristine water ran down into a stream surrounded by mountains on three sides. The sound of the water flowing was soothing, and wildflowers growing along the water's edge added further colour to the landscape.

Suddenly, on the mountain's crest to our left, a large herd of mountain sheep appeared, including some giant rams, and many ewes and their young. Anticipating they would rush down for water, we stayed still, but they had sensed danger. Finally, after about an hour, a young ram impatiently dashed toward the spring and started to drink. My father patiently held the gun, and I waited for his reaction. A few seconds went by, with no movement from my father. After quenching its thirst, the ram quickly rejoined the others. En masse, they disappeared over the crest.

My father usually hunted wildfowl, but hunters don't forgo a rare opportunity, especially mountain sheep, known for their elusive nature and challenging hunt. Surprised and curious, I couldn't hold back.

"Father, why didn't you take the shot?" I asked.

"It was a moment of clarity; there is more to hunting than just taking a shot," he said, his voice carrying the weight of experience and wisdom. "Sensing the risk, the mountain sheep chose not to drink; their survival instincts were strong. The critical point was when the young ram, blinded by thirst, put his life in peril to drink, a fatal mistake. His thirst weakened his judgment, making the hunt unjust and unethical – the skills of the hunter and the hunted were not at the same level."

In that period, despite the Iranian government's modest hunting regulations, my father had many rules and guidelines for himself and us. He always followed special procedures. His respect for nature and moderation was always at the forefront. During our hunting excursions, his ability to inspire was consistent. However, later in life, I refrained from hunting due to my interest in Gandhian philosophy. But in general, my father had an enormous capacity to influence others.

I recall another occasion, hearing someone banging vigorously on our front door one afternoon. When the door opened, a slender man stood there, his face drenched in sweat, his body visibly exhausted, and with an urgent expression.

"I have travelled a long distance by mule and later by car from the heart of the high mountains of Alborz," he said, his voice trembling with determination. "My sister is having complications in delivering a baby and needs immediate help."

As he continued to explain his situation, we became aware that he was a member of a nomadic tribe that moved their herd in the summers to the fertile fields of the Alborz Mountains and in the winter to the warmer regions adjacent to the desert. The mother had been in labour for many days.

The brother's urgent plea to my father underscored the critical nature of the situation. "If you don't immediately accompany me to our camp, she could lose her life."

"I understand," my father said. "We will act right away. Let me contact my physician assistant; he will organize his team to accompany you. Don't worry. He's a fine doctor and will help you."

"No! Please!" His eyes filled with tears, and his voice shook with desperation. "I want you to come with me. We have heard about your work and can't accept anyone but you."

When faced with a serious need, my father never refused to help. He immediately instructed his assistant nurse and another medical staff member to be prepared to depart within an hour.

We left the city around 5 p.m.; the health department's Jeep reached a village at the base of an extensive mountain range. At approximately 1 a.m., on mules, we followed a narrow, winding path. The glow of the moon guided us with its spellbinding beauty as we ascended a mountain for many hours before reaching a plateau. From there, we scaled a second incline. To one side of the path was a vast canyon; on the other, the mountainside.

As we moved forward, in a split second, part of the right front foot of my father's mule went into a hole. The mule lurched forward abruptly to balance its body, nearly dislodging my father. Later, during the daytime, when we returned by the same path, we noticed that the mule had stepped into a crevice created by rain; it was at the edge of a considerable drop. At that moment, if the mule hadn't righted itself, my father and the mule would have plunged hundreds of metres into the canyon.

As the sun slowly brightened the crest of the mountains, we arrived at the camp. I was exhausted. A woman took me to a tent to rest while my father and his team went to the woman in labour. A commotion woke me around 11 a.m., and I asked the assistant nurse what had happened. He told me that after many difficulties, the baby was finally born, and the mother was okay. However, when the husband found out the baby was a girl, he went into the bushes and refused to see the mother and the baby.

"As you know, your father is very sensitive to this attitude. So, he became distraught and asked the brother to go and bring the husband to the tent."

I sat beside my father on a rug that covered most of the ground inside the tent. Many others, including the clan's elders, were seated in a circle. We all waited for the husband to come inside. My father had always fought against backward attitudes, especially cultural tendencies reminiscent of feudal and pre-feudal systems. He was a staunch opponent of sexism. However, considering the prevailing cultural practices of that region, as a first step, he faced the daunting task of convincing the husband and others of the rights of a newborn girl. At the same time, he had to defend the mother from their scorn by debunking many of their antiquated traditions, which viewed women as lesser human beings.

When the husband came in, he immediately sat down with his eyes looking at the ground.

"Thank you for joining us," said my father, asking one of the ladies to place the newborn child before the father. "Look at this beautiful girl. She needs you and her mother; her future depends on both of you." The man hesitantly looked up and turned toward the child; at that moment, she yawned, capturing the father's attention. "Can I respectfully ask you to pick her up and hold her in your arms?" my father asked the man. For a few seconds, complete silence filled the room. Everyone waited to see how the father would react. Slowly, the man's face relaxed, but the faint outline of wrinkles around his eyes was still visible. Under pressure, the father reluctantly bent forward and picked up the child. As he moved her toward his body, their eyes connected. I saw the father's eyes sparkle ever so slightly. "You know, she is part of you," my father said. The man became more receptive and brought the baby closer to his chest. After a few seconds of silence, my father began a conversation with him that lasted more than thirty minutes; also, a few others spoke to support my father. I have never forgotten the expression on the face of the mother when we were about to leave the tent, a look of contentment, vindication, pride, and gratitude.

My fondest memory, which deeply inspired me, was my father's atypical style of receiving payment after examination and diagnosis. As a rule, people were treated differently, depending on their ability to pay. Underprivileged patients paid whatever amount they could afford. Conversely, he was uncompromising but fair with wealthier individuals. They paid the set fees. Also, to preserve the patient's dignity, he had arranged with a local drugstore owner that when he placed an *X* at the top of a prescription, the owner would discreetly inform the patient that a grant covered the cost. Then, at the end of each month, my father would visit the drugstore and reimburse the owner.

Later, I became convinced that when confronting a health concern, the additional torment of dealing with its financial aspect can enormously burden the impoverished. In times of medical need, not being concerned with its cost should be a universal human right, not a privilege. Shouldn't everyone be entitled to a satisfactory level of health? Must we link profit to the most essential human need? If yes, should we pay for the air we breathe or the beauty of nature we observe? I didn't doubt how my father would have replied to these questions.

Throughout our lengthy stay in the United States, my siblings and I occasionally visited Iran during the summers until we completed our education and left the United States separately. During one of these visits, my father recounted an incident while we were away.

"In addition to my duties as managing director of the city's health department," he said, "I was also responsible for the anti-narcotic campaign, which was an educational endeavour. One day, the gendarmerie [a military force assuming police duties beyond the city's jurisdiction] captured two men trafficking a large amount of opium. In those days, the city's health department had to certify the authenticity of apprehended contraband substances."

An influential man with much leverage, who was known to have connections with powerful figures, asked my father to change his report.

"The man said to me, 'I will deliver you a briefcase filled with money in return. I want to caution you that higher-ups are involved. They want the report to show the package contents are not opium; instead, it should say *ghareghoroot* [an extract of milk that looks like opium].'

"It was rumoured that Ashraf Pahlavi [the Shah's sister] was connected to the opium cartel. No one dared to involve themselves in these matters. It was a dangerous dilemma that could potentially be life-changing. So, I informed the man that I needed time to think and would let him know my decision soon. I knew my conscience would not allow me to change the report. Therefore, I had to find a way out of my huge predicament."

After some deliberation, knowing that if he didn't accept their proposal, the cartel would try to block the package transfer to the ministry head office, my father sent the contraband covertly to Tehran. He anticipated that some cartel members would arrive at the train station to intercept the contraband. Despite these risks, he directed his assistant and the department's driver to go further, to the next train station, and from there, the assistant travelled to Tehran. As soon as the head office received the package, they summoned him.

"I knew beforehand that when the package was delivered, for certain, someone would tip off the cartel. When I arrived, it became evident that the head office was heavily infiltrated. Therefore, they trumped up a story against me as a retaliatory action. Their narrative was that I had neglected to follow through with an urgent need of a pregnant patient. They had submitted a signed affidavit from her and other so-called witnesses to prove their accusation."

My father was told to return to his place of work, and in time, they would reveal the result of their judgment. In a few days, it became apparent that the health ministry was squeezed from two sides. On one side, the cartel was pressing for disciplinary action. On the other side, some people in the ministry knew about his work in the region. They recognized that it was wiser not to upset the public. Otherwise, petitions or letters would have inundated them. Therefore, they lobbied hard to bury the file. At the same time, however, it needed to be done in a way so they could save face. The false accusation had serious implications for my father's career and reputation. After some time, he was absolved of the accusation, and the file was quietly shelved.

Following his account, many questions went through my mind. How flexible should he have been when he drew an ethical line and took a stand? Are people correct when they say, "Everyone has a price"? If that's true, why do some people stand up for their beliefs to the point of losing their lives? Could there be something more important than one's life? Is having a moral stance an act of becoming free or an expression of a utopian dream?

Later, I became interested in why many people use words like *idealist* negatively. Looking back on both human history and my own personal history, I realized that ideas believed unattainable at one time evolve and eventually tend to become more realistic. Only when people challenge what previous generations consider socially unacceptable will new ideas find their place in society.

2

My Grandmother

They cannot take away our self-respect if we do not give it to them.
Mahatma Gandhi

Besides my father's enormous impact, a few exceptional people on my mother's side also significantly influenced me. As a child, I remember my maternal grandmother reminiscing about her four brothers.

"The first was an army officer and one of the earliest physicians educated abroad," my grandmother used to say. "He died in a battle with Yeprem Khan [a famous revolutionary in the Constitutional Revolution of 1906]. He fought against the forces favouring Mohammad Ali Shah [the sixth king of the Qajar Dynasty]." It was a period of great upheaval after the Constitutional Revolution. The king unsuccessfully attempted to regain his father's lost power by abolishing the new constitution and the sitting legislature.

Her brother had boldly moved beyond the fortification to break an impasse. Before he could find cover, a bullet pierced his body. Yeprem Khan, witnessing his close friend being shot, crawled out of the trenches to save him. The soldier who shot

Yeprem Khan could have never imagined that his bullet was destined to take the life of a great revolutionary.

"My second and third brothers enlisted in the Ottoman army. The former died in the First World War, and the British imprisoned the latter after the war. My younger brother was the closest to me, especially after my first and second brothers died." Her eyes glistened with tears as she spoke, her love for her brother palpable in every word. "His kindness was exceptional. I could count on him whenever I needed any support. Unfortunately, his immense courage in battle caught up with him, which eventually ended his life."

My grandmother was tall and slim, and her facial features suggested that she must have been exceptionally beautiful in her youth. She was independent and had a powerful personality. Nonetheless, her younger brother's death, in many ways, devastated her. My mother told us that our grandmother never recovered after receiving the news of his death. She always reminded the family of her first and last brothers, their bravery, and how they lost their lives. Her third brother lived a natural life and used to say, "I was never as brave as my other brothers; that's why I am still alive." After the Ottoman Empire's defeat, the English occupied Iran; as an officer in the Ottoman army, her third brother was arrested and jailed in India. He was eventually released due to my grandmother lobbying Vosough ol-Dowleh, the prime minister of the time, and a change in the political climate. He immediately returned to Iran and joined the gendarmerie.

Later, in 1921, he, in conjunction with Reza Khan and three others, and with the support of Great Britain, carried out a coup against Ahmad Shah, the son of the deposed Mohammad Ali Shah, which eventually led to the rise of Reza Khan's Pahlavi dynasty. During Ahmad Shah's rule, the combination of his weakness and the presence of the remnant ideals of the Constitutional Revolution allowed the elected legislators to play an active role in the country's affairs. This semi-democratic climate was a departure from the norm, but the coup brought an end to most of that, significantly altering the political landscape.

I always wondered about my third great-uncle, his part in removing Ahmad Shah, and the coup's role in blocking the movement toward a relatively democratic trend. This progressive shift started in Iran during the mid-nineteenth century and received some life support in the Constitutional Revolution of 1906. The movement primarily promoted democratic values, freer civil society, social and economic justice, balanced jurisprudence, the rise of social institutions from the bottom up, and, in general, the continuous participation of people in their political affairs. In some schools of thought, these ideas are construed as the "software" of development, although at that time, we were and are now very far from reaching these concepts. However, maybe it was a beginning and perhaps an aspirational goal.

Oddly enough, some believe that during Reza Khan's rule, the construction of railroads and buildings and the creation of new departments in government – mostly in name only – constituted a total breakthrough. Their logic makes no distinction between the "software" and the "hardware" of development. There is a significant difference between the practice of democracy and its appearance. When the coup happened, it was as though the life of an innocent child – the infant democracy – was taken away. Perhaps, to start this evolution again, a new "child" must grow once more and live a natural lifespan with all its messiness and challenges.

The bravery of my first great-uncle during the Constitutional Revolution of 1906 and the courage of my last great-uncle – without judging his stance in the subsequent events – have had a significant influence on me. My grandmother's fearlessness, independence, and strong personality also left a lasting impression on me. She was part of a new generation of families that emerged from the periphery of the Qajar court, which preceded the Pahlavi dynasty. These families were mainly educated abroad and had a modern outlook that sometimes bordered on obsessive behaviour or excessive positivism. This outlook reflected the changing times and profoundly impacted my grandmother, making her self-confident but somewhat didactic and imposing.

She was the first woman in Mashhad city to voluntarily not wear a veil in public. She had no problem lobbying the prime minister of the day to get her brother out of prison. Her fearlessness in asserting herself was apparent when people said things or acted in a way she disapproved of. She could sway people to her point of view. However, her demeanour with us was predominantly kind and understanding. She was always our rock and a faithful supporter. As a child, I knew that my troubles and secrets were safe with her. After listening and comforting me, she would speak to me at a level I could understand as a child, encouraging me to find solutions.

In retrospect, when I think of an archetypal liberated woman, her image comes to mind, even though she passed away many years ago. Her way of life taught me the value of being free-spirited and the importance of women's liberation from the grips of dogma and patriarchy. When I imagine an emancipated woman, I think of a strong, independent, determined, caring, and fair-minded woman who is not against men but opposed to the material conditions that create patriarchy – a system that feasts on ignorant men. She ventured toward that goal a century ago.

I remember hearing a powerful account of her from my mother. My grandfather, a married man, fell in love with her and wished to marry her as his second wife. Despite the challenges she would face being a second wife and her personal resistance to the idea, she eventually accepted his offer. In time, she noticed some patronizing behaviours. On one occasion, he verbally demanded that she submit to his will. Without hesitation, she put a gun under her chin and told him that if he moved one step closer, she would pull the trigger. He realized that she was serious and apologized profusely. It took him hours to convince her that he had learned his lesson. To persuade her to put the gun aside, he vowed never again to show any semblance of the same conduct for the rest of his life. On reflection, I don't know if he stayed true to his word indefinitely; nevertheless, knowing my grandmother, he must have tried for some time. Her impact on our family was profound, and her strength continues to inspire us.

My grandmother's self-confidence greatly impacted many, including my mother, who adopted some of her idiosyncrasies. My mother also had an uncanny ability to engage with young people, making them feel secure in confiding their troubles with her. She was resolute but approachable and had a noticeable capacity to accept new circumstances.

Figure 2.1 *Opposite top*
Yeprem Khan (front row, right) and my first great-uncle (back row, second from right) fought together in the Constitutional Revolution of 1906.

Figure 2.2 *Opposite bottom*
Four of the five men who orchestrated the 1921 coup against Ahmad Shah shown here: Reza Khan (far left); Major Massud Khan (front row, second from left); Seyyed Ziaaddin Tabatabaee (front row, third from left); and Colonel Kazem Khan Sayyah, my third great-uncle (front row, second from right).

Figure 2.3
Family gathered for a wedding ceremony in the late 1920s. At the back stands my grandfather (centre) with my grandmother to his left.

3
Validation

Safety is not the absence of threat; it is the presence of connection.
Gabor Maté

Living with my father was memorable, but it had to end once I finished the grade six.

As planned, we joined the rest of the family in the United States, but after some months, my father's leave of absence was over, so he returned to his work in Iran to support us.

A whirlwind of thoughts filled my mind while my mother drove me to school. It was my first day at Portola Junior High School in Orange, California. A rush of anxiety wouldn't let me think straight. *I don't know a word of English. Who will help me navigate my way around?*

The room was full of students. No one noticed me. Many were occupied with their issues. The ambiance differed from that of Iranian classes. The green blackboard looked odd. Colourful posters decorated the wall. One door opened to the front and the other to the back, with windows all along the top and sides of the doors. A tiny US flag stood at an angle about a foot away from the top left corner of the blackboard. Small desks were attached to the seats and placed casually in rows.

I found a place at the back of the class. The bell rang, and everyone took their seats. A middle-aged woman stood up and uttered some words. I was totally at a loss. *What did she say?* Later, I discovered she had introduced herself as Mrs Jardin, our English teacher. Also, from her gestures and the reaction of others, it appeared that she was telling everyone to stand up and face the flag. Then she mentioned something else, and everyone placed their right hand on their heart and started saying things. *What should I do? Should I do the same? Should I remain seated?* I quickly stood up with both hands at my sides to show respect.

They sat down, she said something else, and half the class raised their hands. After fidgeting for a few seconds, I joined those who didn't raise their hands, hoping not to be noticed. Then, everyone brought their hands down. Each morning, without exception, this ordeal would repeat. Numerous students would raise their hands; sometimes the same ones as the day before; sometimes different ones – which was bewildering. To end this constant misery, I raised my hand every other day. It was only months later that I discovered the purpose behind this ritual. Mrs Jardin was taking a survey for the school cafeteria so that they would prepare the right amount of food. All I had done was add an extra count to the list on alternate days.

On my second day of school, after her usual routines, Mrs Jardin turned around, glanced amiably at me, and without any hesitation, mentioned something that I couldn't follow. Her sign language suggested that I stand up. I found myself in a state of confusion, the palms of my hands perspiring excessively and my heart pounding against my ribcage. *What does she want? Why is everyone looking at me? Should I say something?* As I contemplated my next move, I noticed that she pointed at herself and said something I thought was her name. So, I mentioned my name. It was the right move. It redirected everyone's focus from me to the next topic. Later, I discovered she had said, "As our new foreign student, please stand up and introduce yourself."

The beginning of my journey to learn English was challenging, as it was my first experience in another language. The new environment was a constant source of motivation, pushing me to confront and overcome numerous cultural hurdles. As a child, my inborn flexibility allowed me to learn faster with less fear.

My first day in physical education class was unforgettable. All the students had their gym clothes rolled together and a pair of shoes in hand. It was a moment of sheer embarrassment; I had nothing with me. I could feel the heat rushing to my cheeks as I looked at the ground. When the instructor saw the expression on my face, he said, "Here is a list of what you should bring next time."

The list included a reversible T-shirt (one side orange and the other white), orange-coloured shorts, a jockstrap, and a pair of white socks, plus tennis shoes. I was filled with a sense of accomplishment having my new outfit when the next PE class came around. On entering the changing room, I noticed many naked boys suiting up – something I had never faced before. In Iranian culture, it's not customary for men or boys to undress in front of one another. But blending in was more central than anything else, so I joined the others and changed without delay. After the class, we undressed for the second time and took open showers. I don't doubt that my acceptance of this situation would have been more difficult if I had confronted such an anomaly at an older age.

In grade seven, I was the shortest boy in the entire school, except for Mendez – an international student from Mexico who was also learning English. One would think that the challenges we both faced would encourage solidarity. Instead, he seemed intimidated by me, and the rivalry created an unpleasant relationship, my first encounter with bullying. To overcome his provocation and gain acceptance, I tried to make the basketball team, which, considering my height, seemed an elusive goal. But I was sure that if I succeeded, my achievement would shield me from Mendez's harassment. I was delighted when I made the C team, only later learning it was a consolation prize for those who couldn't make the A or B teams. Even though I wasn't successful in basketball, my relationship with Mendez normalized as time passed. He eventually realized his animosity wasn't helping the many challenges we faced.

My mother, sister, and two brothers had arrived in San Antonio, Texas, a year before. When my father and I joined the rest of the family, we drove from San Antonio to Orange, California, where my sister was accepted at a nearby university.

We looked over the Rio Grande as the road drew near the Mexican border. We decided impulsively to go over a one-way bridge to see a busy marketplace where people were selling fruits and other products. We had no idea that this was the border between Texas and Mexico. As we reached the other side of the river, the atmosphere changed – everything looked impoverished. The hustle and bustle of the fruit sellers and the pottery makers were like Tehran's Grand Bazaar. Beautiful clay bowls, pots, urns, and pitchers were on display. Further ahead, others were selling huge, colourful Mexican hats and ponchos covered with intricate stitching.

After an hour of exploring, we decided to continue our trip and nonchalantly drove toward a second bridge that led into the United States. However, this route bore no resemblance to the one we had taken an hour ago. In front of the bridge, we saw a large gate with a border kiosk.

When the guard examined our documents, he said, "You don't have a double-entry visa. I can't let you pass."

We were stunned!

"We didn't realize the river separated the two countries," said my older brother.

With teary eyes, my sister fumbled in her purse and pulled out her university acceptance letter. Handing it to the border guard, she said sobbingly, "If I miss my registration, my entire future will change drastically."

The guard's demeanour softened slightly, but our pleas seemed ineffective. Dejected, we pulled over to the side of the road. Then, out of nowhere, the guard approached us and addressed my sister. In a calm tone, he said, "I've made arrangements with the Mexican authorities. Hurry to the other bridge before their shift changes, and they'll let you drive the wrong way back to the States." The sudden twist of fate left us dumbfounded.

We drove toward the Mexican guard in silence, the tension in the air palpable. He shifted his gaze slightly in the direction of the United States and gave us a nod of approval. We crossed, holding our breaths. As we drove away from the bridge, a wave of relief washed over us, the tension releasing from our bodies. We acknowledged the enormity of our luck. The contrast with the usual US bureaucratic approach was evident, and the guard's empathy was a breath of fresh air.

For several years, I would revisit many aspects of that episode. Why was the border to one side so open and the other side so controlled? Why would the Mexican people relinquish control of their borders and seemingly become submissive to the United States? What are the reasons for controlling borders? Does affluence play any part in the attitude of "us and them," and can it evolve into a quasi-racist sentiment? I became suspicious of the typical argument of having borders. Some claim that borders exist due to a discernible divergence of people's history, cultural background, shared values, language, ethnicity, religion, and way of life – could this reasoning be a pretext? Why are affluent immigrants with different cultures, upbringings, and backgrounds usually accepted more readily? There must be other concealed reasons regarding people's tolerance of others. Could the narrative of border control be used as a slogan to manipulate uninformed individuals, diverting their attention from more pressing matters? Does it have anything to do with protecting the well-to-do's interest? Should we only attribute the stark difference in wealth in one country versus its border country to the intensity of hard work, or were other unjust reasons at play?

As a rule, regime change or luring leaders through financial enticement buys loyalty, which brings about tolerance for resource extraction. This process contributes to the prosperity of one country and the detriment of the other's economy. The people in less prosperous countries naturally want to immigrate to the wealthier countries so that they and their children can enjoy the abundance as well. There might also be other reasons for emigration, like war and climate change, often linked to the insatiable need for developed countries to grow without limit. Ironically, after all this, the rich countries usually claim that their success is only due to the hard work of their citizens. And, of course, their next step is implementing enhanced border control.

After arriving in California, we lived together for less than six months before my father returned to Iran. Not long after, we discovered that sending money to the United States was a long process, with limitations on how much my father could make and transfer. This financial situation left us in a state of uncertainty, underscoring our urgent need for additional funds.

With limited employment options for a twelve-year-old, I became a paperboy for the *Santa Ana Register*. Every day after school, I would fold newspapers, secure them with a rubber band, and place them in a sack attached to the back of my bicycle. On rainy days, I would ensure all the papers were protected in plastic bags. But Sundays were the test: the newspapers were twice the size of a weekday paper. I would rise early to receive them at 6 a.m. and distribute them by 8 a.m.

Occasionally, on weekends, a supervisor would pick up a group of us in the morning to go door-to-door to solicit for the paper. It was an exciting assignment since it allowed me to meet many people from different backgrounds. I was taken aback by the generosity of people in cities like Norwalk, with a heavy concentration of low-income workers. In these neighbourhoods, people were primarily open, a stark contrast to the more affluent communities, where we were usually met with arrogance.

After a while, I joined my older brother in a machine shop as a second-hand operator. He was in charge of the only automatic screw machine in the shop, and my role was to deburr the parts that came from that machine.

Once, I received a big barrel filled with small, narrow stainless-steel tubes to deburr, a daunting task. They were about 6 inches long and ¼ inch in diameter. A giant clock marked time. For four hours, I would deburr parts one at a time and look at the clock every few minutes, hoping the big hand would move faster. Every minute seemed like an hour – I felt like the clock was growing and coming toward me. The repetitive nature of the task was so intense that one day, due to mental fatigue, I lost concentration. The tip of the drill caught my glove. It twisted the cloth so rapidly around my hand that it broke my index finger. After a week of healing, I returned to work, and the same task.

A year later, our mother had to return to Iran and join my father to take care of pressing matters. We were placed with American families through her efforts and the guidance of Dora, the principal's secretary at my oldest brother's school. Dora, a beacon of support and kindness, was instrumental in this transition. My older sister and brother lived with Dora and her husband, and my other brother and I with Karen and Jim. This change required numerous difficult adjustments, but also entailed many exciting and fun activities.

My new foster parents, who had no children, did what they could to create a warm atmosphere. At the same time, Jim believed in discipline. For example, as a fussy eater, I frequently left my meal's last portion.

"Please finish your food before leaving the table," he would say. For the first few weeks, I forced myself to swallow it down. Later, I learned a trick that he noticed but didn't acknowledge. I would spread the food all over the plate and say I was done.

"You can leave now," he would murmur.

I encountered similar rules on other occasions. Nevertheless, Jim carefully balanced discipline and kindness. He was a history teacher but also enjoyed running competitively. My brother and I would frequently run with him for a few miles.

He would often notice our fatigue toward the end of our run and advise us, "Stop running! Start jogging! I'll go ahead and come back soon," he would say, running for a long distance without us. His stamina was remarkable; he would return to us with vigour and alertness. Through his encouragement, we gradually built our endurance and could cover longer distances. He was an excellent role model in many ways. His teachings still resonate with me today, reminding me that when one reaches the point of exhaustion, it's tempting to give up; every moment after that is an opportunity for deep self-reflection and a boost to one's confidence. Triumph is just around the corner when one nears complete exhaustion. The line between excellence and mediocrity may be drawn in the final moments of refusing to yield.

Karen, also a teacher, was kind and understanding. She would often give us kitchen chores so we could work together. Later, I discovered this was her way of creating a closer bond with us. She would go along with some of her husband's disciplinary actions but generally be more lenient.

My American foster family had a swimming pool in their backyard, which we enjoyed during the summer. As a family, we embarked on a trip to Yosemite National Park. The park's natural beauty, with its breathtaking cliffs, towering sequoia trees, magnificent waterfalls, and crystal-clear streams, left an indelible mark on me. The sheer splendour of nature made this trip incredibly memorable. Even now, I can vividly recall its beauty and the joy it brought me.

My older sister and brother lived a few miles from us. We would visit them once every week or so, alleviating some homesickness. However, our home comforts and those weekly visits didn't diminish the gravity of being away from our parents and living in a new country, especially at my age. I remember those days with mixed feelings. Some days were fun and exciting, and others were lonely and sad.

Later in life, I could never be sure which part affected me more.

4

Schooled

The danger of the past was that men became slaves. The danger of the future is that men may become robots.
Erich Fromm

After a year, my mother returned from Iran. The joy of reuniting and creating a shared space after living apart was a sweet solace that filled our hearts. We left our respective American families and moved to a rented house together.

My new job at McDonald's, just a short walk from home, was more than work. It was where a few of my classmates and I met, blending work and play. Sometimes, when the manager was preoccupied during non–rush hours, we'd have lighthearted moments like pickle fights. For a few seconds, the sliced pickles meant for hamburgers became projectiles. After the commotion, the pickles stuck on the porcelain tile walls were collected and placed back in their bowls.

The manager initiated a contest among those assigned to the grill: who could lay twelve patties completely straight with onion bits sprinkled on them in the shortest time? The winner would have their name on the bulletin board until someone surpassed their time. During rush hour, four people were assigned to the grill. But when Bosh and I were there, we could perform more efficiently, putting out more hamburgers than four people. Bosh, a second-generation immigrant from Germany, was an ambidextrous, tall, skinny, blond teenager. Speed hamburger-making was a thrilling challenge that we took to with our best efforts, pushing our limits.

After a while, I could place a dozen patties straight on the grill in six seconds. I took pride in this skill, and soon enough, my name found its place on the bulletin board – an ego booster. That swiftness carried over to assembling the burgers.

"Twenty-four bottom buns are dressed and ready," Bosh would say.

Then, I would put six top buns on the six cooked patties and place them on the dressed bottom buns and with four lifts of the spatula, twenty-four burgers were ready to go. Despite the home office's indifference to our suggestions, performance, and work conditions, which could have spoiled the excitement of any accomplishments, I found joy in being productive.

Only a year and a half later, when I was fifteen and a sophomore in high school, my mother returned to Iran again. My parents thought it was time for us all to become more independent. Some days, I missed her and felt homesick, but other days, I cheerfully looked for new possibilities. My older sister and brother went back to live with Dora and her husband, while my other brother and I went to live with a different American family.

Our new foster father, Ted, was gentle, calm, and patient. His wife, Marylou, was friendly and enjoyed talking with us, which helped us improve our English. We quickly felt a sense of belonging in their home. Ted's outstanding characteristic was his ability to teach with great patience and encouragement. He taught us how to cook and sail. Eventually, we were allowed to sail his Sabot, an 8-foot, 95-pound cat-rigged dinghy, solo in the Newport Bay Harbor area.

I remember an occasion sailing alone. Suddenly, a gust of wind changed the sail's direction, which prompted the boat to pick up speed. Another blast coming from the starboard side jolted the boat. In response, I manoeuvred the boat into a close-hauled position – when the sail is trimmed in tightly and is closest to the wind – which causes the boat to heel and accelerate. It tilted so much that the edge of its deck went in and out of the water. Placing my feet under the hiking straps, I leaned out to balance the boat, which forced me to stretch out my body as far as possible. I had reached the highest speed achievable, though if I had tilted a few degrees more, the boat would have capsized. At that instant, while the water and the air whipped my face, I had an epiphany: there are moments in life when one wrong move or change of circumstance can shift everything from the pinnacle of triumph to failure, causing a free fall into darkness.

As the wind subsided, a serene tranquility enveloped me, soothing my senses as I sailed my small boat across the ocean's enormity. I was lost in contemplation of the immenseness of the horizon and the magnificence of the scenery. The gentle caress of the wind against the sail and the waves thrashing the boat's hull created a harmonious chorus, gradually increasing its pitch. The repetitive pounding of the waves, like a rhythmic echo of a meditation chime, calmed my mind and body.

The sense of accomplishment and Ted's trust in me to go solo was inspiring. Momentarily, I felt like I could sail the Pacific Ocean. This feeling of success fuelled my ambition to excel in athletics during my junior year in high school. I would diligently go to the handball courts every day after school, envisioning myself in the finals of a varsity tennis match. I would hit the ball against the concrete wall until the sun dipped below the horizon. This ritual only intensified by the summer after my junior year. Finally, in my senior year, I earned a spot on the varsity tennis team and eventually secured the second-best player rank, significantly boosting my confidence.

Our senior studies teacher, the tall, laid-back Mr Faskins, asked: "Can anyone name the speaker of the House of Representatives, the minority leader of the House or Senate, and the Supreme Court chief justice?"

My hand was the only one in the air. At that time, my knowledge of US politics was limited; however, I made it a point to stay informed by regularly tuning in to the news.

But in some ways, being good at something wasn't aligned with being accepted. For a high school student to feel accepted by their peer group is challenging in any generation. The issue of cultural integration enormously amplifies this struggle. I noticed that nonconformity was branded as a mental abnormality in some sectors of society. To face this challenge, I tried to join the school's Key Club, a path my two elder brothers had taken. This boys' club aimed to provide service, build character, and develop leadership. It was primarily made up of popular students who were members of the varsity athletic teams. It was a big honour to be accepted, and I am still baffled as to why I was allowed to join. When they gave me the Key Club jacket with its colourful insignia, I wore it joyfully, even at home when no one was around.

In our weekly Key Club sessions, we learned how to conduct meetings using Robert's Rules of Order and how to elect a president, secretary, treasurer, and sergeant-at-arms. We were also responsible for carrying the American, California, and school flags in the opening ceremonies of the varsity football games. Every season, each member would get a turn to march with one of the flags to the middle of the field.

When my time came, I was given the Stars and Stripes to carry, but I needed instructions. So, I decided to follow the boy assigned to the California flag. Everything was okay until we left the field; our last step was to fold the flags triangularly. I had no idea that when doing this, it was considered disrespectful to place the flag on the ground. As soon as I did so, many people sitting on my side of the stadium stood up and began yelling. Eventually, the boy carrying the California flag came to my rescue when he saw my startled face. After that embarrassing mistake, it took me some time to overcome the humiliation I felt. It weighed heavily on my mind, so I tried to be invisible at the next few Key Club meetings.

Looking back on my high school years and the importance of fitting in, I recognized the added pressures most atypical students, including me, face. The system often compels one to give in to the unwritten rules of conduct that the majority follow. It became clear that there was little tolerance for those on the fringes of society. Is it true that in the early stages of development, we learn how to comply so that, in the future, when we shoulder more responsibility, it becomes relatively painless to follow the mandates of society? Schools, as institutions, are often reduced to a training ground for submission and compliance. Being different becomes an enormous challenge, and many must prepare to face its consequences.

After a while living with my second foster family, I started work on weekends in a nearby car wash. My job was to vacuum cars before they entered the automated washing area, completing my task in less than a minute. After four hours of continuous work, we were granted a single break. Dealing with the monotony was a significant challenge at first. However, I soon discovered a fascinating technique: as cars arrived, I aimed to identify the condition and upgrades to the car by looking at its owner. To my surprise, in many cases, people of modest appearance drove remarkably well-maintained vehicles.

One day, my supervisor instructed me to follow him in my car to a strip mall some kilometres away. I was driving an old blue Beetle that I had inherited from my older brother. We arrived at a mall directly across the street from another car wash. He instructed me to park in the mall's parking lot and count every vehicle going into that car wash. As the task became monotonous, I got out of the car and sat on the hood with my feet on the bumper. The car wash manager noticed me; fortunately, before he could react, my supervisor returned. He seemed disappointed that I didn't realize the secretive nature of the operation. Following that incident, I went back to the more arduous task of vacuuming.

After hours of vacuuming on Saturday, my supervisor asked me to clean the public bathrooms. It seemed that the consequence of my mistake did not end with my return to vacuuming. When his order sank in, I felt uneasy. My childhood aversion to unclean things or places posed a challenge. Cleaning these filthy bathrooms became a daunting project. Used toilet tissues were scattered everywhere, the taps were covered with grime as if not cleaned for months, and the toilet bowls were disgusting. I took a deep breath, narrowed my eyes at the mess before me, and decided to hose down all the walls. Then, with great reluctance, I cleaned and sanitized both bathrooms. I couldn't wait to go home and shower. Afterward, I felt a profound sense of relief: I had done something I didn't think I was capable of. Looking back, I realized that by stepping out of my comfort zone, I had gone through a form of therapy that helped me to become less hygiene-sensitive.

While working at the car wash, I began to look for a less demanding job. After a while, I found an ad in the local newspaper for vacuum cleaner salespeople. The ad was enticing; for every vacuum sold, they would pay a commission. It didn't mention any details, only that one could potentially have a handsome income after a week of training. The ad gave the impression that a base salary and a steady job were part of the package. But as I soon discovered, this was not the case. The company knew how to play a psychological game. A young and inexperienced person like me who had invested a week of his time would be tempted to continue. It was as if they knew how to make us believe it wasn't a waste of time. I practised my sales pitch at home. I had a persuasive pitch, but the rejections still hounded me. After one month, I had made zero sales.

As I continued, I couldn't shake the feeling that the customers buying the vacuum cleaner were being misled. The instalment plan and the interest rate meant they paid much more in the long run than if they had purchased a quality vacuum cleaner from a store. I felt a deep sense of anger and mistreatment for being personally deceived. Despite the conflicting thoughts that plagued me, my desire to connect with people overruled my urge to convince them to buy under duress. It didn't take long for me to move on and seek a more fulfilling job. And so, I couldn't help but wonder if the system uses our basic economic needs to seduce and turn us into a subservient, silent army to exploit and be exploited.

5
Becoming

All resistance is a rupture with what is. And every rupture begins, for those engaged in it, through a rupture with oneself.
Alain Badiou

Lying on a warm, sandy beach in California's Corona del Mar, I closed my eyes while a tranquil feeling enveloped my bones. I could taste the remnants of the early morning mist as it gently emerged from the belly of a light breeze. Amid the cry of the gulls competing with the muted roar of the waves, I embraced the calmness of the occasion and eagerly went over my plans for tomorrow's graduation.

Preparing for the ceremony, I knew I had to leave work early. Besides, I had to pick up Sandy's corsage before the flower shop closed. It would be the first time meeting her parents, and I could already hear the barrage of questions they would likely have for me.

The next day, as I approached Sandy's front door, a spirited, attractive brunette with beautiful eyes, I felt a mix of anxiety and joy. My heart raced with anticipation. Opening the door, she moved swiftly toward me, suggesting an immediate departure.

"Oh, hi. Let's go!" she murmured.

What a relief! It appeared that her parents had left early. As I opened the car door for her, she looked at me and smiled, causing an odd shiver down my spine.

In the car, I handed her the corsage. Her eyes gleamed with elation infused with a spark of shyness. She took the corsage from the box, gave it to me, and said, "Can you pin it on?"

Looking into my eyes, she leaned forward and waited. The fragrance from her hair was so pleasant that it momentarily stopped me. I looked from the corsage into her eyes and then back. Finally, trying to be composed, I pinned the corsage to her dress. It's fascinating how, during teen years, euphoric reactions or worrisome moments can be as brief as the flight of an old leaf leaving a tree.

After the ceremony, we headed to Catalina Island to celebrate. This 21-mile-long island is 19 miles from the mainland.[1] We took a ferry and arrived around 9 p.m. The festivities ended sometime after midnight, but the urge to discover the rest of the island kept us from leaving, so we joined another couple under the moonlight and wandered around. As we walked close to the water's edge, the green vegetation surrounded the rocks in such a graceful form that one could imagine them converging into a single entity, amplifying the impression of oneness. As the waves hit the rocks, serenity enveloped my body. When the rising sun slowly illuminated the horizon, I felt a new chapter in my life was about to open. During later challenging periods, I time and again recalled that night.

Sandy and I continued to find joy in our relationship. The thrill of our meetings was always reminiscent of a child's excitement over simple things. We met frequently for over a year, each meeting filled with anticipation. As our relationship progressed, I wondered if it would grow stronger or fade. Gradually, our interests diverged, leading to the mutual decision to part ways.

As a construction planner, I worked the day shift that summer, although I knew I'd resume the night shift in September when university started. My primary job was creating charts for major contractors to manage their projects. In the summer of 1971, I enrolled in the School of Industrial Engineering at California State Polytechnic University, Pomona.

Every evening, I worked until midnight and listened to the news non-stop. It was a tumultuous time. The country was experiencing intense political activism, primarily by young students. Simultaneously, the hippies were searching for a new way of life. They were fascinated with anything that could rupture the present norms. Their foremost aim was to explore anti-establishment lifestyles.

The hippie movement left a lasting impression on many young people, in different ways, me included. However, what really caught my attention was the rise of political activism. While there were some similarities between the two movements, they also had their differences. Apart from the anti-establishment sentiment, the activists' primary focus wasn't so much the abandonment of conventional ways of life; their priority was to bring about political change. As these two trends evolved, my interest in the goals of the political activists grew stronger.

The Kent State shootings and the United States government's involvement in the Vietnam War were pivotal moments that significantly altered public opinion. On 4 May 1970, the National Guard, in an unexpected turn of events, fired on unarmed Kent State University students protesting Richard Nixon's offensive in Cambodia, killing four and wounding nine others. This tragic incident sparked a wave of demonstrations and strikes across the county. More than 450 colleges, universities, and even high schools, with around four million students enrolled, were disrupted by strikes.[2] Surrounded by the turmoil, I pondered the balance between selfishness and generosity. Why should we care? Could we make a difference? Should I join them? I had no answer. Yet, I realized that my mere presence in such a volatile period was transforming in and of itself.

Frightened, the Establishment began a covert campaign that lasted for many years, the primary aim of which was to neutralize the activists through economic and social enticements. Among many schemes, I noticed the expansion of issuing credit to as many people as possible, including students. Credit was often extended without considering the individual's ability to repay on time, resulting in substantial debt accumulation and a long-term financial burden for many. Concurrent with this action, the enticements to buy through the influence of mass media, advertisements, and other means increased. The artificial need for "things" intensified, so people's debt constantly increased. The widespread adoption of credit cards in the mid-1970s established a new norm for many, perpetuating the cycle of debt.

As people consumed more and their expenses mounted, they were compelled to work longer hours and take on additional jobs. In many cases, this financial strain forced other family members to join in. While changes in the workforce encourage independence for many women, unfortunately, the excessive focus on making a living often leaves little time for other aspects of their lives. People in debt generally become overly cautious and more conservative, especially those with heavy mortgages who couldn't risk losing time from long work hours by concerning themselves with other matters. It could jeopardize their status at work or be a reason for their dismissal – they couldn't afford to rock the boat. How would someone living paycheque to paycheque manage their debts if they lost their job?

It was perplexing to see that practically all higher education institutions planned to increase their tuition fees drastically. Year after year, these institutions continued to raise their rates. Neo-liberalism was gaining momentum. The elites were beginning to make record-breaking profits at the expense of others, while real wages started to stagnate. It seemed that the interests of the privileged were moving in the opposite direction from the aspirations of countless students.

In an attempt to neutralize activists, the authorities aimed to reduce the number of students coming from a lower economic stratum. They must have assumed that students who had the means to pay their ever-increasing fees would most likely be less rebellious. As a result, colleges and universities systematically became less accessible to many intelligent young women and men. Sadly, even those who could graduate did so with increasingly massive student loans.

When I started my first year at university, the tuition fees were so affordable that students could cover their expenses by working part-time jobs. However, in the early and mid-seventies, the fees escalated annually.

Other schemes to reduce defiance, such as the termination of conscription in 1973, were most likely part of this plan. This course of action also averted the problem of draft dodgers – many young men resisted the draft; some burned their draft cards and left the country for Canada or other locations. The participation of young volunteers in the latter part of the Vietnam War and subsequent conflicts became more desirable than that of draftees who had never sought army life. I became convinced that, in the eyes of the military establishment, volunteers were deemed more reliable and obedient and less likely to leak damaging information.

Could a one-sided tax structure be a brilliant imposition of a new norm, diverting people's attention from more pressing issues? I pondered whether the tax structure in the United States could entice people to become obsessively protective of their interests and ultimately indifferent. I wondered about the fundamental principles of the tax framework. Why should those living below the poverty line pay taxes? Why do taxes take a good portion of families' income when they are working to make ends meet? Generally, no one likes to pay taxes unless they have reached a level of consciousness that enables them to find a balance between their private sphere and public responsibilities. Could a low-income family taxpayer be more vulnerable to the influence of politicians with different agendas? Can a narrative of "tax cuts for everyone is the solution" be a way to enlist financially strapped taxpayers into the silent army of the powerful without receiving any benefits in return? Could one reason for promoting such slogans be another way to reduce the tax contribution of the wealthy? I became convinced that the voluntary tax reporting system enables the rich to exploit its loopholes. Unfortunately, it also seduces some ordinary people to be less truthful, perpetuating a culture of deceit.

It's a perplexing reality that those who constantly struggle to make ends meet often lack awareness of the root causes of their harsh social conditions. They tend to support ideas that benefit the affluent, who frequently take advantage of them, unwittingly adding to their own misery. Could this essential contradiction, which they often have little insight into, be their biggest challenge? Is this stark inconsistency the most crucial issue for them to recognize?

While these vicious cycles of manoeuvring continued, I sensed that the public had become more engaged in "everydayness" and were distracted from other affairs that significantly affected them. In such circumstances, people became more prone to be politically cautious.

A few months before I completed my bachelor's degree, the executive committee of our university's Persian Club asked me to be the co-master of ceremonies of the Persian Eve celebration. This event was to observe *Nowruz*, the Persian New Year, which begins on the first day of spring. Before the start of the celebration, one of the organizers told me I would be the English speaker for the ceremony. The other emcee, a young Iranian woman, would be speaking in Farsi.

Stepping into the auditorium foyer, I saw many pictures of political prisoners, victims of the Shah's regime. At that moment, a profound sense of admiration came over me. I couldn't help but think of the immense suffering of those who stood up for their beliefs and opposed the dictatorship. It was my first real encounter with such a serious political atmosphere, and it left a lasting impression on me. As I met the other emcee and was briefed about our script, the weight of the event's political undertones became clear. My initial impulse was to be supportive without concerning myself with the consequences.

I was entering new territory, one that required some commitment with a great deal of learning ahead. This event was just the beginning, but the Kent State episode a few years back and other related experiences gave me cause not to be apathetic. I felt the urge to continue with the show with no misgivings. At that time, I didn't know the consequences activists might face. I was deeply immersed in the night's mood and eager to be part of the process.

During this period, I went out with a few girls, but up to this point, they weren't serious relationships until I met Vida. One late afternoon, waiting for an evening class, I went to the dormitory's cafeteria for dinner. I sat at a table near a column that separated my table from another section. Looking past the edge of the column, I saw a girl seated close to the window.

One glance at her took my breath away. Her dazzling profile and the way her hair shone in the light were so mesmerizing that I couldn't look away for at least a few seconds. Then she turned toward me, and her Persian eyes gave her away. Should I go to her? What if she leaves before I gather enough courage? Without overthinking it, I walked confidently toward her table and stood before her.

"Are you Persian?" I asked.

"Yes!" she remarked softly.

"Are you waiting for someone?"

"Yes, I'm waiting for my friend Shohreh."

"Are there many Iranians in this dormitory?"

"There aren't," she replied.

"Can I join you?"

"Okay," she murmured. Her eyes displayed interest. After roughly an hour of chatting about each other's past and present, I asked if I could see her the next day.

"Yes," she said.

Our second meeting was at the same place. Shortly after, she invited me to her foster parents' house. She didn't live with them, but they looked after her from a distance. It appeared that Vida's parents had arranged this from Iran so that she could get additional support from an American family. She came from a wealthy family in Shiraz, a city in south-central Iranian; they were so well off that her parents had paid a girl, Shohreh, to be her chaperone throughout their studies. Shohreh was the same age as Vida and came from a modest family. They were both living at our university's dormitory.

Our relationship progressed until the Persian Eve ceremony. Something changed that night. We walked to the dormitory after that event, our thoughts and emotions stirred by the experience.

"What did you think of tonight?" I asked.

"I don't know – I've never been to one of these places," she replied.

"I haven't either, but it made me think about political prisoners."

"I didn't like their criticism of the government," she said.

"But weren't you taken aback by the Iranian authority's treatment of the opposition?"

"Let's not talk about politics," she suggested. "Let's focus on lighter, more pleasant topics."

We said goodbye, and she went inside the building. Different thoughts swirled in my mind. While there is so much suffering, why would we only talk about happier subjects?

I learned about her plans when I saw her at her foster parents' house the next time.

"I'm going to Iran for the summer break. I need to ask you a question," she said in a serious tone, looking at my surprised face. "You know I come from a conservative family. I'm not allowed to have a long relationship without the question of marriage. Can you have an answer for me soon?"

I looked into her eyes, became silent for a moment, and said, "Let's discuss it when you return. It's an important subject; we shouldn't rush it."

A few days later, she left for Iran. Her departure left a void in me, and our last encounter was a constant presence in my thoughts. I found myself in emotional turmoil, trying to disentangle my feelings for her from the fire the ceremony had stirred within me. Our worlds would have been more aligned a year ago, but now, uncertainty clouded our connection. The ceremony had left an indelible mark on me, and the weight of past events like the Kent State shootings and the United States government's role in the Vietnam War also loomed large in my mind.

A voice inside urged me to call or write her. I pictured a future where we were married: how would her lifestyle blend with mine? Weighing on me was my affection for her and the stark disparity in our upbringings. Was her reference to her conservative family a veiled expression of her feelings? These uncertainties and questions, without clear answers, consumed my thoughts.

It was a difficult summer. I couldn't resolve the contradictions swirling in my mind; they were like a storm I couldn't calm. In the end, I decided not to reach out unless she initiated contact. My hope was that by giving her the power to decide, she would feel less hurt. And so, a relationship that was both emotionally rewarding and painful came to an end.

At that time, I was gradually leaning toward Mahatma Gandhi's philosophy. He believed in non-violent civil disobedience, resistance, and political struggle for self-rule. The word "*Swaraj*" means self-rule, but Gandhi believed that at the individual level, it meant self-assessment, self-purification, and self-reliance. I read about him and those who had inspired him: Henry David Thoreau, Leo Tolstoy, and Jesus Christ. I even looked at the Bhagavad Gita to better understand Gandhi's Hindu philosophy. Given my secular background, his religious leanings didn't appeal to me, but I was encouraged by his political views. Soon, I accepted the non-violent method of struggle and attempted to develop a calm and tranquil temperament. At one point during this transition, I focused on not being angry, and met with some success for three years. I joined a Transcendental Meditation group led by Maharishi Mahesh Yogi. However, the group's exaggeration of the benefits of Transcendental Meditation troubled me so much that I came to question their motives, which in turn contributed to a sharp decline in the quality of my meditation. Ultimately, I abandoned it altogether.

As time passed, I found myself re-evaluating some aspects of Gandhi's philosophy. The most significant shift has been my view toward self-defence. I came to believe that the right to defend myself, my family, my friends, and the innocent was justified, even using force to alleviate suffering.

After completing my bachelor of science degree, I was hired as an industrial engineer in a large orthodontic manufacturing company. My work hours were 8 a.m. to 5 p.m., and I spent evenings taking classes for my master's degree in the same field. I had limited free time; weekends were the only time left for leisure activities: studying, seeing friends, playing tennis, or going out.

I was quite nervous and apprehensive on my first day at work. Prior to my joining, the department had only one senior industrial engineer, Roger Jenkins, an older, reserved man who dressed unfashionably and preferred somewhat outmoded techniques. However, I felt fortunate to be assigned to work with him. He was a pleasant fellow who later became a good friend. His extensive knowledge of our profession was impressive, and he never hesitated to teach me all he had acquired throughout his many years of experience. Despite the age gap, he was open to learning the latest methods from a younger colleague like me.

One of my responsibilities was to evaluate how the workers could enhance their efficiency. Being just twenty-four years old, gaining the acceptance of the older, experienced workers was undoubtedly challenging. To appear older, I grew a beard. I also put in a lot of time and effort to build friendships and dispel the notion that I was on management's side. Unlike most industrial engineers who conducted time studies with minimal interaction, I would start by explaining the study procedure.

This approach helped reduce the workers' anxiety and barriers, allowing me to develop more genuine relationships.

After a year, some employees attempted to unionize; I found myself in a precarious situation. While trying to appear neutral, I knew whose side I was on and how effective collective bargaining can be. Nevertheless, management used a variety of tactics to drive a wedge between the union supporters and the others. These tactics included spreading false rumours about the union's intentions, offering underhanded incentives to those who opposed the union, and creating a sense of uncertainty among the employees. Angela, an intelligent, high-spirited young African-American woman, led the union drive, mobilized many people, and helped generate employee awareness. Her unwavering attempts to unite colleagues to form a collective voice intimidated most authorities. Yet, before the vote, they managed to create a climate of fear that led to management's victory and, subsequently, Angela's firing. Besides the executives' formal power, this episode was a stark reminder for me of their unofficial clout. Eventually, they imposed their will and manipulated many employees, leaving them feeling disempowered and vulnerable.

After a few years, I received a promotion and became a production control manager. At the same time, I was discovering different aspects of Gandhi's philosophy. My friendships strengthened with people who encountered family problems or struggled with an inferiority complex. Recognizing the need for a safe space, I opened my office to anyone who wanted to share their difficulties. This initiative led to at least one or two people visiting me weekly. I was struck by the courage of several women who, despite the societal barriers, were often more open than men in discussing issues and building deeper relationships with others at the cost of exposing their vulnerabilities. I noticed that there were more women experiencing social and family hardships than men. The most common issue was physical abuse by boyfriends or husbands. The second was single mothers struggling financially. As a young man with little experience in relationships, yet filled with passion, I learned quickly that my contribution was to be a compassionate listener.

Looking back at what happened in the factory and my observations, two main points have deepened my understanding of human relationships. First, I saw how the authorities can use their resources to manipulate those less able to resist while, in contrast, others can be creative and show solidarity in finding ways to counter the authorities. Second, I witnessed the injustices that women face. Many women, especially those from lower socio-economic backgrounds, shared stories of being in abusive relationships. In these situations, women often bore the most responsibility for raising children. Unfortunately, the social institutions they needed were often inadequate or nonexistent. Patriarchal norms imposed on them from a young age and a lack of education can contribute to women unintentionally being part of this cycle of abuse and injustice. Instead of being empowered by their family or society to break free from these constraints, they find themselves trapped.

By this time, all my siblings had returned home; I was the last of my family still in the United States and much older. I had become comfortable with the American way of life. Homesickness had changed its meaning since my junior high school years when I had moments of emptiness and loneliness. Now, apart from not seeing my immediate family, the pain of being away from home meant not enjoying Iran's beautiful nature, reminiscent of my childhood, which had left an indelible mark in my memory. The rocks, the trees, and the shrubs felt different. The fragrance of a bush in a valley below the Alborz Mountain range had never left my mind.

In July 1978, I received a letter from my immediate superior that he was planning to promote me to the position of materials manager.

But my mind was already somewhere else. After fifteen years in the United States, I had made a firm decision to join my family in Iran.

6

Returning Home

The desire for possession is insatiable, to such a point that it can survive even love itself. To love, therefore, is to sterilize the person one loves.
Albert Camus

My parents came to the United States for a visit and stayed with me for two months. At the end of their trip, we planned to return to Iran together. I had completed my education and resigned from my job.

It was heart-rending to say goodbye to my colleagues. A single mother with two young children working in the assembly department gave me a letter.

"Please open it after your departure," she said. I later read:

> In times of despair and desperation, to alleviate some of our pain, my children and I discuss and recall the details of my conversations with you. For this reason, before dinner and for as long as possible, we have decided to mention your name in our prayers.

I was overwhelmed with emotion. This incredibly touching letter helped me recognize the value of relationships that enhance compassion and understanding, and the way in which meaningful interactions can change one's perspective. Now, I appreciate platonic friendships more and how they can also be therapeutic for both people involved.

Another colleague handed me a jewellery box with the instruction to open it after my departure. When I opened the box, I found a dime and a letter.

> Anytime you need help, anywhere in the world, use this dime; call, and I'll be there.

His pure and symbolic gift was overwhelming and prompted me to become introspective. Oddly, instead of feeling more self-assured, a sense of humility and unpretentiousness came over me. I felt more grounded.

There was no way of knowing that soon Iran would go through a vast political transformation – the revolution that would change most Iranians' lives. But I was already on my way from Los Angeles to Tehran's Mehrabad International Airport. My decision was driven not only by the pull of family but also by a growing disillusionment.

After receiving my master's degree in 1977, for amusement and interest, I enrolled in another philosophy class offered at my alma mater. In the last days of the course, I shared my decision to return to Iran with fellow students.

"Why would you want to leave such a great life for Iran?" one asked.

I don't doubt that others had the same question but didn't want to ask.

What is a great life? I pondered. *Could only a prosperous life surrounded by numerous trappings and conveniences be the answer? Is happiness only having a comfortable life?*

It became clear to me that having a suitable standard of living, which by and of itself is pleasant, should not be denigrated. However, the fundamental question that arose was whether we, as humans, are intrinsically driven by more than just the pursuit of wealth and power. Do we inherently possess characteristics covering the entire gamut from selfishness, greed, meanness, and narcissism to compassion, kindness, altruism, self-sacrifice, and generosity? I wasn't sure if moving to Iran would solve this dilemma, but I had to break away from the status quo.

Before my flight, I spent my last days in the United States in a blur of reflection. Despite the many conveniences around me, I was driven by a need to understand why I wasn't content and desired a change in my life. What troubled me was the lack of clarity on what a "satisfied life" or "happiness" truly meant. As I observed those around me, I was particularly struck by the sight of individuals who followed others and had resigned themselves to a life of "everydayness," tranquillized with superficial pacifiers.

I was amazed at how consumerism, a culturally sanctioned behaviour, had become emblematic of most people driven by the pressure to conform. I realized that society often instills in us a perception of being immensely small and powerless in the grand scheme of things, leading us to believe that our primary role is to be a first-class consumer and trust the multitude spins the authorities frequently feed us. Above all, I was baffled by the public's love of purchasing and their lack of attachment to the product itself, which made the need to use the object morph into a lower priority.

Furthermore, the act of buying can serve other purposes, such as seeking prestige or alleviating temporary despair. Perhaps, before long, we become indifferent toward what we buy due to the alienating schemes of those who control the market.

So, to fill a void, consuming becomes a psychological anodyne. In time, this feeling of indifference could also harm our relationships. Even love or friendship might become expendable. Ultimately, all bonds could become fragile.

I became convinced that the system demands a type of "success," defined in terms of stepping on others to gain a higher status, not the kind of experience that I valued and received from the people I worked with who had once been strangers to me. Instead of accentuating our better characteristics, which could resemble co-operation, empathy, and kindness, the system encourages us to expose our worst attributes, like self-interest and egotism. As soon as one capitulates to the pressures of the circumstances, one becomes the means for propagating selfish traits. I realized that the benefits of conformity are too enticing to underestimate. Conversely, we are frequently reminded of the challenges that accompany nonconformity. We become conditioned to think that societies can't organize themselves in any other way than as they are now. This myth is relentlessly hammered into our psyche, so we don't think for ourselves. The fear of change becomes the fear of relinquishing privilege. Ultimately, there comes the point in our lives when we must either follow the painless path, with its status and benefits, or follow the beat of a different drummer with all its consequences.

I was compelled to understand my aversion to the view of so-called social Darwinism, a notion that erroneously ties the theory of survival of the fittest to human social behaviour. This connection has long been debunked and is antithetical to Darwin's and Wallace's theories. Can we genuinely accept the argument of the powerful that it's natural for the strong to dominate the weak? Conversely, is there truth to the assertion that primordial humans protected their weak to ensure the survival of the group? Is there an inherent satisfaction in helping others? Humankind has struggled with these philosophical questions for ages.

I kept drawing together the themes in my philosophy texts. Eventually, and after some time, by convincing myself that there might be an explanation, I found refuge and maybe some answers in Albert Camus's insightful book *The Myth of Sisyphus*, giving me a new window into this dilemma. His analysis showed me that the world's absurdity, due to the contrast between an irrational universe and the rationality we seek and impose, can perhaps be restrained by three powerful words: revolt, freedom, and passion. A rebel is a man or a woman who says no to an act – they resist when an action crosses a line. By saying no, they evoke a value that brings a need to say yes to something contrary. This value can make life worth living. By realizing the world's absurdity and revolting against it, we become free to live a passionately enjoyable existence.

At the time of my departure, I acted primarily through instinct. I made a solemn vow to myself, a commitment that would alter the course of my life. I pledged to change my lifestyle drastically and never return to a superficial life.

As my parents and I flew from Los Angeles International Airport to Boston to visit a cousin on our way back home, I was struck by a news article about a tragedy in Abadan, Iran. This incident took place only days earlier, on 19 August 1978. A gang of thugs had set fire to the Rex Cinema, and the resulting blaze had claimed the lives of approximately 377 people.[1] The shock and horror of this event, the senseless and tragic loss of life, deeply affected me. Due to the growing resentment against the Shah, the popular belief in Iran was to blame the regime. They felt that the assailants must have had ties to the regime, although this belief was never corroborated. However, some Iranian historians have suggested that the non-secular opposition to the Shah could have been involved in this act of violence.

I saw my siblings when we entered the waiting area at Tehran's airport. Following a warm reception, we all went directly to my parents' home and celebrated our reunion. It was the first time in many years that our whole family was in one place again. Holding back happy tears, I glanced over at our family pictures on the credenza, which took me back to my childhood, the trips with my father, living with him for a year, and flying together to the United States. The memories flooded back, and I found myself lost in the past, reliving the moments we shared. After fifteen years, having lunch with them was unusual, but in a good way. I had forgotten the remarkable taste of my mother's cooking – my taste buds had a tantalizing reunion with her food. We discussed life in Iran and our experiences, and it felt like we had never been apart.

As the country's mood rapidly changed, hoping to quell the public's discontent, the Shah implemented reforms. And so, in August 1977, Amir-Abbas Hoveyda, the prime minister of Iran for over thirteen years, was replaced by Jamshid Amuzegar.[2] Nevertheless, due to people's persistent pressure from below, he didn't last long and was forced to resign within a year. My arrival in August 1978 coincided with the appointment of Jafar Sharif-Emami as the new prime minister. The streets were filled with protests, and the air was thick with tension. It was a challenging time to return home.

Conversing with my father was always a unique experience. He wore his heart on his sleeve when discussing the current state of affairs, particularly the people's uprising and his life after we left him. As the former head of the health ministry of a province, and though retired, he had a deep personal stake in the issues we discussed.

"I can't imagine how hard it must have been to work with the central office in Tehran," I said, my voice filled with empathy.

"The regime's rampant corruption and nepotism was out of control," he said, his voice heavy with the emotional burden of his experiences. I could feel the weight of his words, the frustration and disillusionment, the anger bubbling beneath the surface. "So much so that work wasn't rewarding anymore. The difficulty for people like me working in the Shah's bureaucracy was having a job that helped people while working for an unscrupulous government."

"Could you do anything about it?"

"No, the rot was too acute," he murmured. "I had to isolate myself to survive."

The extent of the demonstrations and resistance surprised him. He couldn't fathom the possibility of toppling the Shah's regime with so much support from the West – military, intelligence, economic, and technical support. Yet, he couldn't hide his pride in seeing people's daily progress in resisting repression.

In less than ten days, I found myself at the centre of a massive movement. Many people would demonstrate in the streets daily, shouting slogans against the government. In response to the protests, Jafar Sharif-Emami named a new Cabinet to appease the crowd. His government promised several changes, but the atmosphere was so explosive that people rejected the hastily drafted reforms. Consequently, day after day, the political climate became more radical. As this volatility grew and transformed the country, my desire to get a feel for the situation deepened. I visited different areas of Tehran, mingled with demonstrators, and discussed their demands. It was not just a massive learning process but also a journey of personal growth.

One demonstration – a powerful display of unity – involved about a million people. We had marched for hours without food or water when a demonstrator entered the crowd carrying a flat piece of bread called *sangack*, about 75 centimetres long and 35 centimetres wide. We handed the bread one to another, each breaking off a small piece before passing it on. No one took more than a bite. The prevailing zeitgeist spurred on many questions, and my mind was spinning, watching this happen. A seemingly trivial act revealed a more profound phenomenon to me. It sparked thoughts about the potential for positive change in human behaviour during extraordinary times. Could the social temperament and conditions in a specific period be so motivating that people en masse would no longer be indifferent? Can people who in solidarity with one another strive toward a perceived purpose become more enthusiastic, less selfish, and overall better individuals? If good and bad traits exist within us, can exceptional conditions amplify one trait over the other?

The demonstrations were only a sign of things to come.

7
Revolution

Pessimism of the intellect, optimism of the will.
Antonio Gramsci

As the protests persisted, the government declared martial law at midnight on 8 September 1978, the 17th of Shahrivar, the sixth month of the Iranian Solar Hijri calendar. All demonstrations were deemed illegal, which set the stage for a tragic turn of events. With many unaware of the martial law, people poured into the streets around 7 a.m. and the crowd advanced toward Jaleh Square. The army's response was swift and brutal, resulting in the death or injury of hundreds. This violent reaction from the military marked a decisive shift in the struggle against the Shah. It was a defining moment for the movement known as Black Friday. On that day, I was a few kilometres away. However, some people had seen the massacre and informed me of the details. I was amazed at how the army could fire on Iranian citizens with so much cruelty. My first encounter with such brutality since the Kent State episode, it was one incident out of many tragedies to come.

The regime lost control of the situation without considering the political climate. The government thought the protesters would return to business as usual if they showed force. Instead, the unrest spread – into labour strikes and, most importantly, among the oil refinery workers. The demand became the removal of the Shah.

At the same time, the economic impact of the strikes changed conditions so much that the continuation of the status quo was no longer an option. And so, the leaders of the United States, Britain, France, and West Germany met in the French territory of Guadeloupe in early January 1979.[1] They concluded that Mohammad Reza Pahlavi – the Shah of Iran – could no longer maintain the West's interests and needed to go. Accordingly, on 16 January 1979, he left Iran and went into exile, creating a vacuum that paved the way for Ayatollah Khomeini's return. He was born in Khomeyn – a city in the central province of Iran – in 1902 and spent his early life in the seminaries of Qom and Najaf. His political journey began in 1963, and his opposition to the Shah led to sixteen years of exile.[2] During this time, he conducted his political activities mostly from Najaf, Iraq, and later, in the suburbs of Paris, France. In 1979, he returned to Iran and was proclaimed by the new constitution as Founder of the Islamic Republic and Supreme Leader.

His arrival on 1 February 1979 marked the beginning of an all-encompassing historic transformation. Everything changed, and the transition of power had commenced. However, as an observer, one peculiarity that struck me was the stark contrast in the political climate of 10 February compared to 11 February.

On 4 February, Ayatollah Khomeini appointed a shadow government. As a result, for seven days, two governments existed concurrently. Before leaving the country, the Shah had appointed Shapour Bakhtiar as prime minister. When 10 February came around, I noticed that most of Ayatollah Khomeini's appointees were acting strangely – events did not go according to plan. A prime case in point was the beginning of this day. It was early in the morning when the army re-implemented martial law. In response, the shadow government announced that people should adhere to the law and leave the streets. Yet, I witnessed many people who did not observe the order. Later in the day, when developments grew out of their control, the shadow government changed its stance to maintain leadership and directed the people to resist the regime's martial law.

One theory, mainly supported by certain segments of the Iranian political intelligentsia, suggests that during negotiations with the West, the West demanded that the army remain intact after a new government was formed. The rationale was to rein in the future government by relying on the military as a counterforce. However, Western negotiators did not anticipate the deep division between two factions of the army. They believed the wing loyal to the Shah would eventually yield to the side favouring the West. Everything changed when the former attacked one of the air force barracks and encountered resistance from the lower-ranked soldiers sympathetic to Ayatollah Khomeini. By 10 February, the armed forces were so torn apart that the religious and non-religious opposition only accelerated the army's collapse. This theory explains why the army was already weakened physically and psychologically before the opposition attacked the barracks. The opposition's strike was one more blow to a beleaguered and overwhelmed army, which had limited capability to withstand further assaults. The tenth of February marked the turning point, leading to the army's dissolution as a force, creating substantial confusion for the shadow government. This confusion, a result of the sudden power vacuum, was the reason for their initial indecision. After 10 February, events took a completely different turn, drastically altering the political atmosphere in favour of the shadow government. Many of us witnessed the implosion of an army expected to act as a counterforce. Consequently, the shadow government emerged as the dominant power throughout the country and, by default, became an interim government.

At that time, many citizens had picked up a gun from the barracks and felt responsible for protecting their city. I, however, was engulfed in a personal struggle, unsure why I didn't take up arms. Perhaps my non-violent past influenced my decision. So, on the fateful day of 10 February, I drove frantically to the hot spots, my focus on looking for as many wounded as possible. The urgency of the situation drove me forward.

As I looked out my car window, I was captivated by a young woman holding a Kalashnikov. She seemed to be guarding a strategic building. Her radiant black hair fell to her shoulders from the edges of a beret, a checkerboard bandana covered the top of her dark-green army jacket, and her pant legs were tucked tightly inside her laced army boots. She apparently belonged to a guerrilla group that had just come out in the open. Her presence represented a significant cultural shift, a fascinating aspect of the era, totally incongruent with the region's cultural history of women. In general, women were brought up either traditionally or in a pseudo-modern culture, which had gained a foothold in the mid-twentieth century – one can possibly trace the inception of both cultural behaviours to the imposition of structures of power, which create divisions at different stages of history. The possibility of both upbringings being apolitical – one concerned with religion and the other with consumerism – seemed likely, particularly the latter, which during the last part of the Shah's regime had been significantly influenced by the rise of consumerism. However, the volatility of that period had become so acute that, as a rule, preconceptions of an activist's typical behaviour would generally turn out to be erroneous.

International movements played a significant role in influencing Iranian dissidents. The Cuban Revolution and other similar insurgencies undoubtedly impacted the guerrilla movements of the time. After the 1953 *coup d'état* against Prime Minister Mohammad Mossadegh, "many" Iranian activists gradually shifted from traditional opposition to militant activism. "Most" were passionately strong advocates of self-sacrifice and pursued high standards. However, despite their aspirations, some in the secular movement, including women, were influenced to an extent by the mainstream norms and mores, guided by various power relations throughout history. Even though they claimed to be opposed to the dominant culture and envisaged themselves as entirely on the fringes of society, they weren't wholly immune to its pressures.

With the passage of time and before the advent of mass demonstrations against the Shah, signs of strategic and tactical change in most opposition groups began to emerge. It all began with a serious discussion among different factions regarding the effectiveness of their armed struggle against the Shah's regime over the years preceding the 1979 events. A predominant opinion emerged that its efficacy as a strategy had become questionable. Gradually, and especially after the revolution, the political views of several groups began to evolve. Their idea of militancy changed. Except for a few groups, the concept of armed struggle began to fade even as a tactic.

The country's historic transformation created a palpable climate of excitement and dynamism in the first days and weeks after the revolution. The continuous emergence of new ideas

Figure 7.1 *Top*
Black Friday, 8 September 1978, when the regime massacred numerous demonstrators in Jaleh Square, Tehran. The protestors believed that the army would not fire, which proved to be fatal.

Figure 7.2 *Bottom*
A protester's attempt to befriend an army officer, a common strategy designed to counterbalance the army's dominance and unite some soldiers with the demonstrators.

Figure 7.3
An Iranian revolutionary woman in front of Tehran University gate. This image captures the moment of victory against the Shah (10 February 1979) and epitomizes the strength of the people, particularly the Iranian woman.

was infectious, fuelling a sense of anticipation and energy. However, this initial fervour gradually waned, coming to a halt altogether.

Day after day, while relishing the blossoming of novel events, I found myself on a personal journey, determined to understand the impact of domestic and international movements on the masses, the daily changes I witnessed, and the potential future scenarios. This determination fuelled my hunger for information, which bombarded me from all directions. Reading material was now available, in stark contrast to the Shah's regime when it was banned – sadly, it didn't last long. So, I committed myself to reading about the contemporary political movements in Iran and abroad.

For nearly a year, I was immersed in the vibrant discussion circles of the University of Tehran's courtyard, where diverse opinions clashed and merged. I participated in numerous discussion centres, each a melting pot of ideas, where the day's most pressing issues were dissected. On one such occasion, I witnessed a heated debate among the young and old: What fate should befall the captured elements of the Shah's regime – execution or imprisonment?

"They deserve to die!" said one older man, his voice trembling with emotion. "Just think of the last twenty-six years of the Shah's despotic rule and how many bright young individuals went to the gallows or were shot. These people were part of the system and carried out atrocities."

"No!" a younger woman cried out, her response with fiery passion igniting reactions. "Killing breeds perpetual violence. When will this vicious cycle end if we act like the previous regime? There is a difference between revenge and justice. Hopefully, in time, we might forgive a person, but we can never forgive and forget their action or the system that brutalizes people. If we believe in justice, we should have them rightfully adjudicated and sent to prison if convicted."

Her daring statement took me aback. I knew the captured individuals had committed acts of brutality, but I felt more comfortable with the young woman's point of view. I now regret that I didn't forcefully back the young woman. Unfortunately, the crowd overwhelmingly sided with the older man; understandably, their emotional state was extremely hostile toward the Shah's regime.

Later, my takeaway from that discussion and other events was a profound realization that the zeitgeist of the time sways people in directions such that contemplating alternatives doesn't gain traction. These same individuals in different circumstances could reconsider their decision. Only a few with leadership qualities can defy popular opinion; however, convincing others at that time and place would have required a monumental effort from that young woman.

I was amazed at the speed with which books were translated and introduced to the public and how quickly they were sold. A few days after 11 February, while walking across the street from the University of Tehran, I noticed that in front of many bookstores or other shops, white cloths were placed on the sidewalk, held down with a rock or a brick on each corner. On top was an assortment of books. These cloths with their wares were spread out for almost half a kilometre. Most pertained to political issues, but a full spectrum of subjects was displayed, from secular left to religious views. What was truly inspiring was the vibrant sight of people reading in parks, universities, and other places, actively engaging with the new-found freedoms. The increase in demand due to abandonment of censorship (albeit ultimately temporary) was astonishing.

Amidst the abundance of books, a spirit of experimentation emerged alongside the creation of organizational reforms. Establishing civil institutions also became a priority, coinciding with the operational resumption of most factories, universities, government offices, private companies, and many other organizations. This period saw the emergence of student coalitions, workers' unions, syndicates, co-operatives, cultural associations, academic alliances, NGOs, and other organizations, each embracing a new mandate. These civil institutions flexed their muscles and sought their place in the new power structure. Political parties or groups also began to appear. Some previously considered illegal during the Shah's regime surfaced from the underground and overtly started their political activities. Simultaneously, the political landscape became more dynamic with the establishment of new parties and groups, attracting members and contributing to the diversity of the societal changes during this period. These political groups covered the entire spectrum, from left to right and religious to secular.

Philosophically, most Iranian secular opposition groups mirrored an international political movement interspersed with some homegrown interpretation. For example, groups to the left of the spectrum entertained various versions of the world's left political view, from guerrilla units who believed in armed struggle to non-violent groups who aspired to and pursued parliamentary engagement. However, most of these latter groups were inspired by and acquired their plan of action from the experiences of other countries, which in some cases posed challenges and proved to be too different from the social conditions in Iran. Many religious groups initially aligned with the regime. However, some groups moved away from the regime over time and became part of the opposition.

In the early days, I recall some officials grumbling about women not covering themselves when away from home. Given the overall atmosphere of that period, it was startling. We had no idea the government would intrude extensively on people's private lives by dictating what they should wear publicly. As a result, many women and others in the big cities who believed the government shouldn't intrude into their personal lives felt a dark shadow over their freedom of choice. Many women in Tehran felt compelled to demonstrate in front of the Ministry of Justice. I volunteered to be a driver for these protesters in order to help in some capacity, along with many other men who were determined to resist this blatant violation of personal rights. The inspiring and powerful role of women in leading this resistance was a testament to their agency and determination. We were completely unaware that this was just the beginning. Over time, I realized that the key to liberating our region from despotism is through the emancipation of women. It must unshackle itself in three domains: the family, civil society, and the government.

A newly born society goes through mistakes and achievements to find itself. However, a complex problem can only be realized through careful examination and recognition of its primary aspects. It was alarming to see how high-ranking individuals or members of a few opposition groups – secular and non-secular – would oversimplify complicated situations. It's famously said, "For every complex problem, there is a simple solution that is wrong." Unfortunately, since credulous people are the most likely candidates to accept simple solutions, they were the first to be recruited. Their unquestioning obedience made them excellent followers, further exacerbating the existing conditions.

Several decades after the revolution, I noticed that many Iranians had an odd view of that period, especially those too young to remember it. Interestingly, some of these individuals were neither supporters of the previous regime nor captivated by the consumerism of the West. I realized that many of them used certain terms, such as "*armangara*" (idealist) and "*roshanfhekr*" (enlightened thinker), disparagingly, conveying a negative connotation. This shift in perception and its sociopolitical implications became a matter of curiosity and concern for me, as understanding its reasons was crucial.

Although the opposition's deficiencies might have had some role in shaping this perspective, I was curious to understand why it had become so widespread. I wondered who was primarily to blame for the bulk of the shortcomings. How would the scale tilt when comparing the miscalculations or mistakes of the more sincerely motivated opposition with the government's repression, having all the resources at its disposal? A brief review of the twenty-six years leading up to the revolution, including the events after the 1953 coup against Prime Minister Mossadegh, might provide a better understanding.

Prime Minister Mossadegh's election and confrontation with the Shah was one of the most significant events in contemporary Iranian politics. He came to power through a relatively democratic process – a rarity. The post–World War II atmosphere was also a contributing factor. His focus on the Iranian national interest rather than partisan and self-serving matters separated him from many others. Unfortunately, his conviction and persistence conflicted with the interests of many internal and international players. Therefore, in 1953, a US- and British-backed *coup d'état*, orchestrated by the CIA and MI6, was coordinated, which eventually toppled his government.[3] And Mohammad Reza Pahlavi was reinstated as the Shah of Iran.

After Mossadegh's downfall and in the lead-up to the 1979 revolution, the Shah's regime violently and vigorously suppressed opposition. This was evident in the frequent executions right after the coup and at various intervals. In addition, censorship, restriction of public discourse, and other forms of repression were implemented. In contrast, the clergy were granted far more latitude and fewer restrictions. This allowed them to use the mosques as primary centres for organizing and mobilizing the masses, a critical factor in their eventual rise to power.

The clergy were clearly the most prepared and ready to fill the void created just before and during the 1979 revolution. They became the leading candidate to assume power, especially considering the Cold War and the West's favouring of the clergy, who had given numerous signals that they had no appetite for or sympathy toward the secular left. When signs of change were on the horizon, for the most part, the left-leaning opposition groups were not prepared logistically and organizationally; most had lost at least their first- and second-level leadership. Hence, the theory raised years later that there were serious alternatives to the clergy who could take power didn't seem realistic to me. The argument was that the opposition had squandered their opportunity through mistakes or miscalculations. However, this way of thinking didn't consider all the factors that led to the clergy's assumption of power. On the other hand, if the internal and external forces hadn't acted so quickly to stop the continuing social transformation by expediting the power grab, then time would have given the left-leaning opposition a chance to become a realistic contender.

Through my experiences gained after the revolution, I've come to realize that despite the mistakes made by the opposition, many members showed a great deal of passion and genuine desire to make a positive impact. While passion alone isn't sufficient, it is an important factor that shouldn't be ignored. There is a significant distinction between those who aren't afraid of the blazing fire and those primarily concerned with ensuring their safety.

I've come to believe that the opposition's underestimation of the government's capabilities was a significant misjudgment. Some factions tended to disregard individuals with traditional lifestyles and underestimate their intelligence. Due to mutual animosity, their perception of a foe influenced their mindset to such an extent that it became difficult for them to acknowledge the opponent's intelligence.

In addition to underestimating its adversary, the opposition needed to assess the political situation accurately, requiring a deeper understanding of the local and global socio-political relationships. They had endured the Shah's authoritarian rule and censorship, where political reading materials were hard to come by – those who attempted to acquire them ran an enormous risk for themselves and their families. As the power struggle between the Islamic Republic of Iran and the opposition continued, it became apparent that the balance of power was shifting in favour of the authorities. In response, the opposition needed to unite and mobilize, which required deep analytical ability, independence, wisdom, and humility. At times, it was also crucial to think creatively and see things in shades of grey rather than black or white. Unfortunately, with the opposition's many built-in historical disadvantages, it was unsurprising to see some weaknesses in these areas.

Years after the revolution, with the repercussions still ongoing, I wondered whether certain opposition groups truly grasped the relationship between achieving a goal and its end result. It's important to understand that the end does not justify the means. Using a misguided process to achieve a goal can have a significantly negative impact and create a destructive culture, rendering the end result irrelevant, regardless of the worthiness of the cause. To avoid the pitfalls of dogmatic thinking, it's essential to remain critical of oneself and others. Those in power can afford to make mistakes, but one mistake can pose an existential threat to the opposition.

I later realized that people in power muddy the water by creating a climate of fear, mistrust, and intimidation, making an accurate assessment of the past more challenging for most, especially for those too young to remember. Ultimately, considering the limitations of that period's more sincere opposition groups, casting judgment on their decisions can be an arduous task for the most part.

The zeitgeist of the time significantly influences our decisions. With our present knowledge and experience, can we fairly judge past actions? One should not have the right to pass an unconditional verdict when examining the past. This is especially true when the particulars of history are interpreted differently depending on our political perspective. History doesn't repeat itself. We can only gain knowledge from its aftereffects. So, I found myself pondering whether some of the critics of the past, armed with the same knowledge and experience as their predecessors, would fare any better than the more sincere activists of that time. We mustn't overlook the fact that this cycle doesn't end with us. Future generations will have the same advantage in evaluating us as we have enjoyed previously. Besides, it's imperative to acknowledge that time changes perspectives and previous "facts." Therefore, our assessment of the past becomes increasingly complicated.

What if, over many years of "cool deception" and propaganda, the government and sympathizers of the old regime managed to create a new version of historical events from before and during the early years of the revolution? Is it possible that over time, to avoid having the spotlight shone on them, the authorities wanted to shift the focus from their economic mismanagement, corruption, and dictatorial rule by emphasizing the opposition's shortcomings? Is it likely that by influencing information, they engaged in a systematic and subtle attempt to change narratives, ultimately leading to distraction and apathy toward politics among many people? Did their distorted version of history alter the meaning of words like "armangara" and "roshanfhekr"? Could this skewed account eventually create a negative connotation in the younger generation's lexicon? It became evident to me that with the emergence of a new zeitgeist, it is essential and constructive for civil society to question past events. However, these questions must be posed independently, free from the influence of authorities and others who may have ulterior motives.

As time passed after the revolution, in conjunction with the government's determination to establish its authority, many pressure groups sprouted to rein in social transformation. It was widely believed that they were funded by some factions inside the government and possibly circles outside the country. These groups mainly targeted the opposition by disrupting most newly established discussion groups, gatherings, organizations, and institutions.

It wasn't just these pressure groups that were shaping the post-revolution landscape; it appeared that other actors were also involved. A theory that gained currency in intellectual circles suggested a more intricate picture. It theorized that alongside the government's attempt to tighten its grip, the Cold War compelled the West to have a vested interest in offsetting the rise of the left.

The Islamic Republic of Iran consolidated its power through domination and force, a process that continued for years in which the prevailing faction chose to eliminate groups with differing viewpoints. They first removed those from outside their domain and then purged elements from inside. As they gained more power, a concerted effort was exerted to impose their way of life on others. They had surmised that an open society posed a danger to their lifestyle and could threaten their survival. They favoured a path that ignored the benefits of mass participation of all segments of society. However, history has shown that in developing countries, mass participation is the best way to fend off the influence of Western forces for economic and political gains.

Later, after a considerable change in the political atmosphere, marked by successive attacks on gatherings, books, institutions, different groups, and civil liberties, I reflected on the significance of an authentic open society and its effects on developing enlightened thinking. How could this social construct contribute to people's awareness, empowerment, and maturity to compel the top of the hierarchy to remain accountable to the base?

Living through the Iranian Revolution was a riveting experience, as I witnessed the chain reaction that led to a complete social mutation – however temporary. Shortly before and after this period, many people overcame their apathy and fear in the face of the rapid and intense transformation of society's social and human condition.

The revolution's early days and the newly blossoming social order did not bring about the blissful political change people expected. Even in those very first days, signs of this development deteriorating were becoming apparent. As time passed, bit by bit, hope for any open society began to erode.

Several years after the revolution, surprisingly, in some segments of the society, it became popular to cling to the past, especially the old Persian Empire and its glories, even idealizing Reza Shah as the saviour of the Iranian people. I was curious about the reasons behind these sentiments. Perhaps the people promoting this narrative had become so biased that they couldn't objectively reflect on the past. They may have overlooked that Reza Shah hindered the development of democracy and the culture it requires. I wondered if, when frustrated in their daily lives, without the awareness of how to vent their frustration, people turn to nostalgic explanations as a way out. To justify their feelings, they choose stories that soothe their anger. Unfortunately, in fitting a narrative to their perceived reality, some people feel compelled to oversimplify the historical complications of the past. Could these distractions aid the Islamic Republic in diverting people's attention from more pressing issues?

That said, a simultaneous act of rebellion took place against the regime's efforts to control – evidence of unwavering determination and inspiring resilience. A non-aggressive and subtle pushback from below emerged as people experienced domination from the top of the pyramid and through governmental institutions.

One form of rebellion was the growing interest in learning to play musical instruments. This trend spread widely throughout the country, leading to the proliferation of music schools. Despite the government's subtle attempts to discourage the practice by deeming non-religious music education unnecessary, many parents, motivated by their children's passion and their own determination, enrolled their children in these schools.

Another act of rebellion was the transformation of the movie industry. After the revolution, numerous original and creative films emerged that spoke of various social inadequacies. Yet, to avoid censorship, the scripts were typically veiled in ambiguity while revealing nuanced complexities.

However, the most far-reaching example of social pushback I witnessed was how many women wore "provocative" headcovers or clothing. Gradually, wearing fashionable and embellished attire without being too obvious became a method of resistance and a way to say no to the authorities. The women became more creative when the government tried to crack down on this behaviour. Their resistance, marked by its peaceful nature, was a testament to their perseverance and grit; yet when faced with government aggression, they responded with patience, waiting for the right moment to counter peacefully. There is a strong argument that, after the revolution, this form of dissent was one of the most extended forms of rebellion against a non-secular system.

As I worked to establish myself in Iran again, to reacquaint with my family and find work, I wondered what new circumstances I would have to accept.

8

War

It is forbidden to kill; therefore, all murderers are punished unless they kill in large numbers and to the sound of trumpets.
Voltaire

Being away from home for fifteen years was too long; adjusting wasn't easy. My Farsi language skills were at the level of a sixth grader. Despite being back for a year and reading Farsi books, I felt uncomfortable and hesitant to speak, fearing I would make mistakes. This feeling fuelled my determination to read more, write more, and put myself in situations that required me to talk more. However, this journey wasn't without its emotional challenges. The feeling of being an outsider due to the language barrier or facing unfamiliar cultural practices was particularly poignant. I was especially conscious of my spelling. Although what is learned during childhood comes back quickly as an adult, it was an unfair contest compared to a person who'd come of age in Iran.

Aside from the language barrier, I had to navigate unfamiliar social norms. For instance, in Iran, I had to readjust to the custom of *tarof*, where accepting something you desire (such as food or other items) when first offered is considered impolite. This was a stark contrast to the United States, where, after observing other children, I quickly learned to do the opposite and accept things when first offered.

After a while, I noticed the differences in the two societies more clearly. One significant contrast was between individualism and a modified form of collectivism. While family structures in the United States and Iran were and still are strong for the most part, there are some divergences. In the States, extended families usually live far away due to the rapid economic development that gained impetus in the nineteenth century and continued. This economic development encouraged people to move in pursuit of better opportunities, making it difficult for extended families to live in close proximity. Even if they lived close by, work conditions were usually so intense that they were often too busy to support each other.

Furthermore, individual freedoms in the United States are generally considered more significant than collective well-being. However, in Iran, due to the overlap of feudal culture (more aligned with religious beliefs) and modern culture (parachuted in by the West and influenced by the North – the old Russian Empire and, to some extent, the time after its downfall), society has a mixture of the two. Therefore, one sector of the Iranian community continues with its support network – including the extended family – and the other sector is gradually moving toward a limited type of individualism. However, Iran's historical collective culture is too strong to fade away in the foreseeable future.

After a short period, the advantages and disadvantages of Iranian collectivism became more apparent. One strong point is that it reinforces people's bonds and creates an atmosphere more conducive to caring and potentially creating. For instance, when older people reach a stage in life where extensive care is required, it's customary for the offspring to arrange a plan to look after their parents rather than sending them to nursing homes, which is inherently a less compassionate environment. Yet, I also noticed its limitations, which became most evident during my interactions with individuals outside my immediate family: for example, the intrusion of others into one's personal affairs, which I observed to a lesser degree in US society. However, the potential for US individualism to atomize people, making caring for others a lesser priority, was a point of concern. Reflecting on the attributes of both communities, I wondered whether we are biologically programmed to organize ourselves as did the early humans, who innately lived collectively to survive. Would a community that values individual freedom within a collective spirit reinforce our better traits and be superior to Iranian and US societies?

After the revolution, Iran experienced a unique relationship with religion, influencing its government, politics, legal system, and socio-economics. Unlike the United States, where corporations have significant sway over the government, in Iran, religion plays a primary role and is an essential component of the government. An example of the intersection of politics and religion is the role of the Supreme Leader. As a religious figure, he wields substantial power and authority over the government. However, this does not diminish the presence of other economic and ideological centres of power, which also exert influence, adding to the complexity of the political landscape. In Iran, religion is not just a part of politics; it's intricately intertwined with divergent views, relationships, and other factors, creating a complex web of interactions that shape the religious and political landscape.

With its distinct characteristics, religion in the United States is also deeply ingrained into the social fabric, political system, legal system, and institutions. It is expressed and embedded differently in urban and rural life as well as in various parts of the country. Notably, the southern and central states are culturally dissimilar from the eastern and western states. And so, religion manifests in complex and multi-faceted ways, requiring a nuanced understanding.

Additionally, an essential difference between these two countries is the profound impact of large corporations in the United States through their substantial financial contributions to major political parties. Their economic might empowers them to leverage their influence and take advantage of the government, other institutions, and the public.

One commonality I noticed between the United States and Iran, as well as individuals universally, is the innate need to gather in official settings such as churches, mosques, group meetings, or other institutional assemblies. Our collective nature compels us to seek out others and feel a sense of belonging. While this camaraderie can yield positive outcomes, it's crucial to realize that due to the authorities' clout and control, they may also exploit and use it to their advantage, thereby creating many followers.

I decided to look for a job. While scanning the employment section of a popular newspaper, an advertisement caught my attention. A large factory in a city I had never visited sought an industrial engineer. I called the number in the ad, and by chance, the staff immediately connected me to the managing director. He was interested in my professional background, which led to a lengthy discussion. At the end, he asked me to see him that same afternoon. I glanced at my watch. It was 9 a.m.

"I'm going for an interview and will be back late afternoon," I told my mother.

Having been away for many years, I found myself in unfamiliar territory when it came to the location of many Iranian cities. However, I had a hunch that this particular one was close to Tehran. As my car reached the outskirts of Tehran at around 10 a.m., I was sure that in no time, I would see a sign indicating my destination. Eventually, I arrived at a city, pulled over, and asked a passerby to show me the way.

"The place you are looking for is another two-hour drive," he said.

Finally, I reached a decisive point – a fork in the road. It was here that I first saw a sign bearing the name of the city I had been looking for. Though it was still 90 kilometres away, the mere sight of its name filled me with anticipation and excitement.

As I contemplated my upcoming interview, the scenery en route captivated me. Its serene, tranquil effect transported me back to my carefree childhood days. It gave me the same sense of peace and calmness that I relished during my father's hunting trips. It was a reminder of how deeply childhood memories, even after so many years, can influence one's state of mind. To my left, a majestic mountain range stretched toward the southwest. These semi-rocky mountains presented a vibrant mix of scattered shrubs, cypress trees, protruding rock formations, and remnants of snow. As the sun played hide-and-seek with a band of clouds nearing the mountain's crest, patches of purple shadow drifted toward the east. To my right, wheat fields blanketed the landscape. The entire valley resembled a sea of light-green waves swaying gently in the breeze. Lost in the beauty of nature, I was suddenly jolted back to reality by a sign: I had arrived in the city.

It was late afternoon when I checked in with the managing director's secretary. I sat in the waiting room, somewhat apprehensive due to my overdue arrival. Ten minutes passed, then the phone sounded. After a short exchange, the receptionist opened the door to his right.

"Please step inside," he said.

I saw a middle-aged man seated behind a large desk. A conference table formed a T-shaped design with his desk. Two sofas faced each other on the other side of the room, with a coffee table in between. The man behind the desk got up, came toward me with a kind smile, and shook my hand.

"I'm the factory's managing director," he continued. "This is Mr Serinath," he said, indicating a man seated on one of the sofas. He was part of an advisory delegation from India and specialized in industrial engineering.

When we sat down, I explained the reason for my delay. As the managing director listened, Mr Serinath began his interview in English. Our conversation lasted for about thirty minutes. At the end of the interview, the managing director asked me to start work in two days. My task was to rebuild the industrial engineering department. Also, I was to receive a small apartment as my living quarters.

Two days later, I returned and checked in with the factory administration. Our department had one receptionist and four industrial engineering assistants. In less than three weeks, we placed an ad for several engineers, and after many interviews, we hired five.

After strengthening our department's capacity, we were now ready to accept various assignments. However, it didn't take long to notice that we were mostly alone. Management was too busy trying to solve their political issues and had little time for the factory's day-to-day technical concerns. So, we identified the main shortcomings, including plant layout, material handling, quality control, inventory control, manufacturing processes, and organizational relationships.

As we examined some of the plant's sub-factories, I realized that a parallel organization, the Islamic Association, affiliated with the government, competed with management and had enormous power. During our industrial engineering work, I became increasingly acquainted with many employees and became known as one of the secular engineers.

While seriously occupied with the factory's technical work, I also witnessed massive regional volatility. The threat of war gradually appeared like a dark veil enveloping the country. Likewise, the sabre-rattling of influential people on both sides became an added provocation. War would usurp ordinary people's safety, which posed an enormous risk to their lives and livelihood. In contrast to the factions that fuelled the fire of confrontation, many hoped this conflict would not escalate. Unfortunately, this whole process changed from rhetoric to action. My fears came to fruition, and a full-fledged war erupted. In September 1980, Iraq's Saddam Hussein initiated a long-drawn-out war that lasted almost eight years, in which both sides sustained massive casualties. Later, it became evident that the United States played a significant role in encouraging and arming Saddam.

After a considerable decrease in American influence and the implosion of the Shah's army, many believed that the West was looking for a way to downgrade the previous regime's substantial military buildup. This theory held that the Iran-Iraq War could, at the very least, weaken the new regime's military power and, at most, deliver a decisive blow to the revolution.

Several Iranian cities became targets for Iraqi planes, creating an atmosphere of fear. In a short period, the war generated scores of refugees. They came from cities that were either occupied or substantially destroyed. These people found sanctuary in other, safer cities, including where I had recently settled.

In response to Iraq's offensive, the Iranian government mobilized, rallying as many people as possible to fight. This was accompanied by a surge of religious and patriotic fervour that swept across the country, fuelling the authorities' recruiting movement. As people signed up for military training, I noticed that the trainees were predominantly from the lower socio-economic sector. It's bizarre: the well-to-do instigate wars while the poor are sent to die.

9
Volunteer

The general population doesn't know what's happening,
and it doesn't even know that it doesn't know.
Noam Chomsky

Within six months of the war starting, our factory called for medical volunteers to serve at the front. Five employees signed up, including three from our department – our receptionist, another industrial engineer, and myself. I had some first aid know-how from living with my father, but I didn't consider myself qualified to do anything more than help a nurse. I had done the same with the injured during the early days of the revolution.

Looking back, it became imperative to recognize my primary motivation for volunteering. Conceivably, I needed to show myself that I could act in times of peril and had the fortitude to participate in some form of resistance against aggression. Due to the government's propaganda suggesting that only religious people resisted Iraq's assault, I felt I had to illustrate that secular people also dared to step up. I was further encouraged by knowing that many others like me were doing the same.

Even though I had moved away from some of Gandhi's beliefs and was critical of certain aspects of his views, his influence on my daily conduct was undeniable. I found that my role as a medical volunteer resonated with my nature and history on an emotional level, a realization that sparked self-reflection.

Was I attempting to rationalize the reasons for my volunteering? Were there other motives behind my decision? In the end, I wasn't sure. All I knew was that, instinctively, to be at peace with myself, indifference wasn't an option. I wondered about the rationale behind the human desire to volunteer for dangerous endeavours. Where does the impetus that spurs people forward come from? In a crisis, what is the driving factor that encourages some to be calm and responsible and others to be panic-stricken? Why does any belief system cultivate motivation, irrespective of the value judgment others might impose? The best facilitator in overcoming obstacles is the presence of a purpose in life. Such a purpose could, in time, change slightly or drastically. Yet, its significance at the time of awakening is profound. Search for meaning can alter how we understand compassion in times of suffering.

In the early spring of 1981, our factory team embarked on a journey to Ahvaz – a city under attack and about an hour's drive from the front line. The factory provided two drivers and their respective cars; they were to drop us off and return immediately. Before our departure, the drivers had gone to the plant's health centre and received various badly needed drugs and equipment. Surprisingly, at the outset of our trip, we were oblivious to the details of our duties. Our only information was that we would be assigned to either a nurse or a doctor when we reached the front lines. We drove all day toward the country's southwest, filled with anticipation and uncertainty.

It was the latter part of the afternoon when we entered the city of Dezful, where we stayed the night, hoping we would be on the road early in the morning. We arrived in Ahvaz the following day and reported to the appropriate centre.

Our team included two other people from our department: Nima and Raha. Nima was a young, highly social, United States–educated industrial engineer from Ahvaz. He had a solid and compassionate desire to help others. Upon joining our department, he quickly became a close friend and a trusted confidant. Raha, our department's receptionist, was an extremely ambitious young woman whose enthusiasm for making a difference was impressive.

After going through some formalities, we were shown to our quarters. Following a short rest, we went to an adjoining hospital to find our next destination. This place was a hub for dispatching medical personnel to the front. We entered the hospital and asked for a doctor who had been in contact with the factory and knew of our arrival. He gave us a quick briefing and a tour of the hospital. Then he told us that the women would stay in Ahvaz and the men would go to Susangerd, a city near the front lines.

The next day, our drivers were getting ready to head back to the factory. At the same time, a soldier gave three of us a ride to Susangerd. The third person was a man from the scheduling department. The lush green vegetation was delightful as we drove through the farm fields. I felt surrounded by nature's beauty and couldn't help but notice the stark contrast in scenery between the south and north of Iran. Fields of wheat, vast and endless, stretched as far as the eye could see, separated by small ridges of earth. The distinctive palm trees of the south added to the picturesque landscape.

Suddenly, it crossed my mind that farther ahead, I might encounter scenes of devastation in similar countryside that farmers had also painstakingly developed. Even more repulsive was envisaging young soldiers from both sides lying motionless on ravaged fields. Some distance ahead, the dreary, opaque clouds felt like a warning. They appeared like a murky veil, casting darkness over an area most likely epitomizing horror. The contrast between the clear sky and the gloomy, overcast atmosphere ahead was stunning. The incompatibility between my present feeling of serenity and what I might soon encounter became the focal point of my attention.

The driver broke the silence by saying, "We are now on the outskirts of Susangerd."

A few minutes later, he directed our attention to his right with a sweeping gesture, guiding us toward our destination.

"That's Susangerd Hospital," he whispered.

He dropped us off at the main entrance. As we entered, I saw a man sitting behind a small desk. I asked for the head of the hospital.

"Follow me!" he said. Before long, he murmured, "He's in that room."

We knocked, and someone said, "Come in!"

When we entered, Dr Eghbal, a middle-aged man, greeted us warmly. After a brief conversation and an overview of our responsibilities, he asked a staff member to give us a tour of the hospital. Despite the hospital bearing the scars of the ongoing conflict, it was cleaner than expected. We visited each room, witnessing the conditions and challenges faced by the patients and staff.

During the tour, we were gravely informed that the war was escalating. Saddam's forces were positioned to the northwest, west, and southwest of the city. In some areas, they steadily advanced while facing fierce resistance, highlighting the urgent and dangerous situation.

The following morning, Nima and I joined an ambulance assigned to the front lines. As we approached, we heard increasing explosions, though we couldn't discern whether they were from mortar, tank, or artillery shells. The sounds grew louder and more frequent. Suddenly, I saw a large orange flash of a fireball to our left, followed by a deafening thud. It was so close that bits of dirt and mud rained all over our car. In a state of sheer panic, the driver pressed the gas pedal so hard that I could hear the engine roar. My heart was pounding, and I felt an adrenalin rush. In an instant, we sped away. Later, I learned that the explosion was so close that the mortar fragments had travelled diagonally higher than the height of our car.

In time, the explosion barrage abated, coinciding with our arrival at the trenches on the front line. In those days, earth was bulldozed into an elevated mound that extended down the line of defence to protect the soldiers. We stopped at the command area and placed a wounded soldier in our ambulance. While the medic commenced his preliminary work, we talked briefly with a commander called Dr Alborz. He expressed concern.

"The situation is dire," he told us, his voice trembling with distress: "I foresee an imminent all-out attack."

Once we secured the person wounded on one side of the ambulance, we continued ahead to check other areas of the front line. Some distance away, we came to the aid of another wounded man, placed him on the other side of the ambulance, and drove back to Susangerd. It was my first encounter with war, where soldiers from both sides came face to face, not more than 200 metres apart. It was a sickening sight, seeing how all peaceful options were set aside so that many young men would die here. My fear and my purpose were in a constant battle. Tears welled up: I had the luxury of leaving this forsaken place, but they were condemned to stay. How were they dealing with their fear, and who would die today?

The next day, one of the hospital supervisors summoned Nima and me and asked us to remove some dead soldiers from a pickup truck that had just arrived from the front lines. We were to place them on a stretcher and take them to the cold room.

"I'll go up on the truck and grab under his arms," Nima said. "You hold on to his legs."

"Okay," I said. "Let me put something on the stretcher to prevent blood stains."

After removing several bodies, Nima murmured with anguish: "I can't look at this body! His chest is riddled with bullets! It's impossible to count the number of shots in his chest."

We emptied the truck and decided to take a lunch break.

"It's hard not to think of the mutilated bodies," I said. "I've never transported bodies." It seemed a gross understatement.

"I wonder if, after a while, it becomes an ordinary task, a new normal?" Nima said.

"It's incredible how one adjusts when faced with extreme circumstances," I said.

"I wonder if it's a way of diminishing psychological harm so that a subconscious coping mechanism kicks in," Nima said.

Later, while eating lunch, I asked Nima, "What's this fragment on your pants?"

After a closer look and visibly disgusted, he said, "I think it's a tiny bit of human brain matter."

I removed it with a spare knife from the table, and we reluctantly continued with our lunch.

Later, after seeing many corpses, my mindset shifted. I became less sensitive, which made me feel guilty. I'm certain my reaction, although accompanied by a significant amount of uneasiness, echoed my extraordinary situation. Under normal conditions, one would have responded with outright revulsion.

That same afternoon, Nima and I, along with a volunteer driver, were assigned an arduous task. We were to transport a fighter who had extensive injuries to Ahvaz since the facilities in Susangerd could not accommodate his situation. Making matters worse, all the ambulances were dispatched to the front lines. We had to relocate him using a pickup truck. His condition was so critical that time was of the essence. His right foot was nearly severed from his leg, and his throat was punctured.

Our trip to Ahvaz was estimated to take one hour. We placed him in the back of the truck. While I held his right foot so he would feel less pain, Nima attempted to support his upper body and head to make the truck's movements more tolerable. His body bore the scars of war, and his eyes reflected the trauma he had endured. For him and us, every moment of the trip was agonizing. Each time we went over a bump, it was so horrendous that the anticipation of the next bump became almost unbearable. His situation was critical; he could have gone into shock anytime.

As I looked at his face and the excruciating pain he was enduring, I began to wonder if it was by chance that young individuals like him wind up in such predicaments. Why aren't the instigators of such wars and their children dispatched to the front lines? Why do we become callous toward human life by internalizing narratives that benefit others? When will such cover-ups get exposed to those who suffer the most?

An hour later, we reached Ahvaz. A nurse pronounced him dead as we stepped into the hospital's waiting area. It's a strange feeling when one's intense care for someone, a care that has forged emotional connection, is instantly rendered useless. Especially if it's a matter of life or death. Yet, when reality shatters those emotions, we have no choice but to carry on. After a few moments of regaining composure, we readied ourselves to return to Susangerd.

While driving back on the same road, we spotted a temporary military post we'd apparently passed. We hadn't noticed it before due to our intense preoccupation. Out of curiosity and as an excuse to rest, we stopped and walked into one of the tents. For the first time in my life, I encountered a prisoner of war – a terrified young Iraqi soldier seated on the tent's floor with his hands tied behind his back. As soon as our eyes locked, I felt a sense of empathy and compassion. I saw another human, just like us, who was no different from us. The word "enemy" seemed alien and out of place. He was probably compelled by circumstances to be at a particular time and place, just like others from "our" side. I couldn't comprehend the captors' hostility and victorious temperament. Their animosity toward him gave me a distasteful feeling.

Later, while reflecting on that scene, I pondered the lasting impact of my face-to-face encounter. Did this intersubjective relationship force me to recognize that the other is like me, acts the same, and commands its conscious life? I felt as if, by meeting my gaze, he was responding to my call. Simultaneously, experiencing this gaze gave me a profound sense of being alive and responsible. The memory of that encounter has never left me, and I often wondered about the fate of that prisoner: did he come out of this ordeal alive?

A day later, a trembling eight-year-old boy arrived in the emergency room, held in his father's arms. His right hand was wrapped in a blood-soaked rag after a mortar shell shattered it. While the boy was shaking uncontrollably, Nima noticed his clenched left hand. He tried to open it, but the boy held on tight. The sweat on the boy's face, his squinted eyes and taut cheeks spoke of his intense pain; yet, except for faint moans, no cries escaped his lips. The weight of a lifetime of suffering had forged resilience within him. I noticed his ragged clothes and shoes as he lay on the bed, covered with blood. His skin, tanned from the harsh sun, bore witness to his impoverished life.

As soon as the doctor became available, the boy was rushed to the operating room. I couldn't help but notice the father's tear-streaked face, his worn-out slippers, and his tribal attire, stained with blood. His connection to the land was evident in every movement as he stood lost in thought, staring at the floor. His weathered appearance was a testament to years of hard work. The deep wrinkles on the back of his neck, the lines on his forehead, his sun-kissed skin, and the calluses on his hands and feet all spoke to the hardship he had endured. When he finally looked up, Nima and I tried to comfort him.

"How can he work without the use of his right hand? He's my only son. Who will take care of me and his mother when we get older?" he asked us.

After nearly two hours, they wheeled the boy out of the operating room. His right hand was cut off at the wrist. Nima knew the region's custom – all severed parts of a body must be ceremonially buried.

"I need to give the severed hand to the father," Nima said quietly to a nurse. After a few minutes, the nurse brought the hand wrapped in a cloth with traces of blood. When the father received it, his face lit up with gratitude.

"Thank you," said the father mournfully.

The boy, heavily sedated, was slowly regaining consciousness. The thick black stripes under his eyes were a stark reminder of the excruciating pain he had endured. His other hand remained tightly clenched. I inquired if he had opened his hand during the operation.

"No, not once," the nurse responded.

Nima looked at me and said, "It's strange, with all this pain, why he won't open his other hand. Whatever is in there must be important to him."

The father, his love for his son evident in his teary eyes, came close to his son's bed, kissed him on the forehead, reached into his pocket, and grabbed a coin. The boy's fingers moved as he attempted to take the coin. Suddenly, in his palm, the first coin shone into view.

The next day, the hospital was in chaos. The air was thick with the pungent smell of blood and antiseptic, and every room and hallway was filled with the moans of the wounded. Even the morgue had reached capacity. The front line we had visited earlier had been breached, and as the units were forced to retreat, other fortifications beyond the city also collapsed. Consequently, defences were mobilized at the perimeter of the city.

I spotted Dr Alborz on a stretcher in the hallway among the wounded. When the volunteers left him, a nurse ran to his side. A few seconds later, I approached him and found that a bullet had penetrated his right lung. The examining doctor ordered his immediate transfer to the operating room. But before he was moved, he looked into my eyes as if he wanted to say something. I brought my face close to his mouth and listened.

"My worst fears came true. After you left, they attacked us with full force," he told me softly.

I placed my hand on his left shoulder and said, "You'll be okay." Even though I didn't fully grasp the severity of his condition, I tried to offer him some comfort in that moment of uncertainty.

Tragically, a few minutes before he was to be wheeled into the operating room, he died.

Many soldiers needed immediate surgeries. Most had to wait. The nurses were frantically going through initial procedures to prepare the injured for their operations. They were also prioritizing the wounded according to the severity of their injuries.

My background as the son of a medical doctor and the year I spent living with him while my mother and siblings were out of the country provided me with a unique perspective. Witnessing some of his operations, I developed a greater tolerance for gory scenes. However, what I encountered during this intense period was beyond imagining. Despite this, I felt compelled to continue assisting the nurses, always mindful of my medical limitations.

While Nima and I were hard at work, we were alarmed by the peculiar behaviour of a fellow from our factory. He was pretending to be a nurse and was caught probing a soldier's large wound below the knee. We rushed to his side, trying to prevent him from causing further harm. Thankfully, the vigilant medical staff noticed his action, which forced him to stop. To this day, I remain unsure of his intentions. Perhaps he was trying to impress the hospital's management. However, this incident was a clear indication of his character to us.

We worked most of the night, the tension in the air palpable. The sounds of tank and artillery shells grew louder as the sun rose, and they were getting closer by the hour, danger looming larger with each passing minute. A whistling noise preceded each blast, and we could gauge the bombardment's proximity by the loudness of the whistles. The hospital trembled with each explosion that slammed the yard close to the building. The atmosphere became so unsettling that the staff was rendered utterly ineffective.

As I listened to the stories of the wounded entering the hospital, it became apparent that we were on the verge of being surrounded.

"They were penetrating our defences from the west, southwest, and northwest," one soldier recounted. "Even when I got nicked, I didn't want to retreat, but my commander pulled me back. It was a moment that tested our resolve."

I remember the reaction of two young female nurse assistants when the possibility of being captured by Saddam's forces became evident. They were standing in the hallway beside Nima and me when suddenly we saw one of them resting her upper body on the wall and sliding down to the floor. The other was showing extreme signs of anxiety. As we went closer to help them, I noticed they were hyperventilating and nearing a complete panic attack. We alerted one of the nurses for assistance. He administered medication, which had some comforting effects. Considering our impending plight, at that moment, I felt a deep connection with our female staff and could understand their added fear and anxiety. Unfortunately, in wars, to humiliate and demonstrate power, women's bodies can become a battlefield.

With every passing hour, the tension grew. Anticipating countless shells pounding the hospital while continuing to work under these conditions took a toll on everyone. Meanwhile, we were receiving more and more wounded. The workload became so overwhelming that cleaning the blood from the floors became difficult. The explosions seemed to be focused on the hospital, suggesting the possibility of an active fifth column within the city walls. Suddenly, the engine room got hit, causing a part of the hospital to go dark. Fire and smoke filled the west wing, but a few individuals reacted quickly and extinguished the fire. Fortunately, no one was injured, and the auxiliary motor was activated, restoring power to some parts of the hospital. As the siege continued, the situation became so intense that the medical staff had no choice but to halt all surgical procedures.

Amidst the crisis, I wondered why we tolerate such extreme catastrophes. Would people with moderate means also protect their interests so intensely? I was amazed at how rigid dogmas effectively create a herd mentality. Is it true that when profit is the ultimate goal for most human endeavours, society's essential needs and well-being often become an unintended consequence and a fortuitous outcome? So, in pursuit of profit, suffering can become sanctioned and rationalized. I became convinced that reducing suffering is the pinnacle of ethics and the only criterion for assessing the essence of morality. Any narrative incorporating this concern in its philosophy must be the nearest to reality.

During these crucial moments, observing people's behaviour became perplexing. I noticed that many were paralyzed by fear, while a few demonstrated boldness. Could this again reflect their ability to define their purpose, regardless of its logic? Does this intentionality foster determination and passion? Can we deal with fear differently when a cause is involved? These difficult questions became a constant presence in my thoughts.

In any event, it must have been evident to many that Nima and I avoided the religious ceremonies. Perhaps by inference we were marked as secular volunteers. They might've reached this conclusion much earlier, maybe shortly after our arrival. Consequently, this created an uphill struggle for us. We knew that without the co-operation and acknowledgment of others, our effectiveness in making a difference would vastly diminish.

We needed to gain the respect of the more reliable people, especially when it became apparent that individuals with different goals and aspirations were in control in places of authority. The religious extremists were on one side of the spectrum, and on the other were people who only appeared religious. Although the latter projected a compliant demeanour, they were hostages of their circumstances. Therefore, with such a diversity of characters, the possibility of piercing their biases was difficult. However, I was convinced that to create legitimacy and indispensability, one had to demonstrate a higher degree of discipline and courage. I also realized people were more inclined to look for charismatic leadership in trying times. I was fully aware that embarking on such a journey was undoubtedly an ambitious task. I wasn't sure I had what it took to meet this challenge.

While looking for an opportunity to improve my relationship with the hospital personnel, a chance presented itself. I found a way to build a connection with an influential individual named Solatty. He had made a name for himself as a reliable and courageous person by supplying the front lines during dangerous situations and, most importantly, had never declined a volunteering assignment. Gaining his respect would have greatly improved my standing with the hospital staff. I felt that he also wanted to test my courage. The assault on the hospital had reached its peak.

"Would you like to go to the southwest corner of the hospital?" he asked me quietly. "I need to retrieve a part for one of our ambulances." The risky nature of the task was evident in his tone.

Without hesitation, I said yes.

10
Chaos

To act is to be committed, and to be committed is to be in danger.
James Baldwin

In no time, Solatty and I were on our way. Since this corner of the building was closer to the line of fire, we undoubtedly increased our chances of getting hit. As we approached this unit, explosions landed all around the hospital's vicinity. Still, neither of us showed any reaction. As soon as we entered the foyer, a new barrage started. He walked a few steps ahead, entered a room, and urged me to follow.

"I found the spare part," he shouted, his eyes darting around the room.

After observing him, it became evident that this trip was a pretext. A few seconds passed.

"If we wait it out, the bombing might subside," he said, his voice trembling with uncertainty. Usually, the bombing would let up and then start again at varying intervals.

Mindful of surroundings, we each found a chair and sat in opposite corners. A deluge of whistling noise was followed by myriad nearby explosions, breaking loose bits of plaster from the ceiling, each bomb a terrifying prelude to the next. After the roars subsided, a tense silence filled the room. We exchanged glances, each waiting for the other to break the silence. The desire to leave was evident, but neither of us was willing to be the first to flinch and say the word. We endured the heaviest bombardment and the most challenging situation for ten minutes. Then, it got quiet for a few seconds.

"You ready to go?" he asked, friendly and co-operative.

Clearly enduring this ordeal with Solatty was significant since I subsequently noticed a change in behaviour from the others.

When we returned to the hospital's main ward, the urgency was palpable. Two more soldiers were brought in on stretchers, adding to the already overwhelming situation. They were placed close to a doorway, hindering the flow of traffic. The hospital had reached a critical point, with supplies running dangerously low and the threat of encirclement looming large. The new arrivals were promptly given potent sedatives to alleviate their pain. People moved chaotically, not knowing what to do, and any further incident could potentially tip the balance.

With Dr Eghbal's help, we arranged a meeting with all the hospital personnel. Fortunately, the staff who knew the nearby terrain were also in attendance. Next, one of the locals who had been in regular contact with the city officials gave us his latest report.

"Karkheh River is behind us, and the Iraqi army is advancing from the other three sides," he said quietly, trying to hide his uneasiness. "Unfortunately, there are no safe bridges to cross nearby."

It appeared that the Iraqi army had planned to encircle the city by land, leveraging the river to complete their siege. They were on the verge of sealing off all land access points, intensifying the pressing nature of our predicament.

We had to act swiftly. There were unsettling rumours that if the city were captured, the lives of at least some of the injured in the hospital would be in grave danger. As we weighed our options, an older man came forward.

"There is a small dinghy about a kilometre from here," he said as he looked at Dr Eghbal. "There are two wooden poles on each side of the river connected to a rope. One must grab the rope and pull the dinghy across the river."

"It's easy," said a local staffer, his confidence bolstered by experience. "I've crossed the river with it a few times."

"No, it's too risky," said a nurse, his bottom lip trembling with concern. "Iraqi soldiers might have occupied the roads by now."

"We have two choices," I said, looking at the nurse. "Stay here and hope for something miraculous to happen or give the river a chance."

"I believe our best option lies with the river rather than leaving our fate to the turn of events," Nima declared, his lip curling in unwavering determination.

After a heated debate, nearly all agreed to accept the older man's suggestion: we would transport the injured and the hospital staff across the Karkheh River and beyond. The river was about 150 to 200 metres wide, and there were more than sixty-five people involved, counting soldiers and civilians. We had to act swiftly before the encirclement was complete; any delay would mean our access to the river would be cut off. After a lengthy discussion about approaching the river, we realized that the only viable option was from the back of the hospital, through a narrow pathway; cars would have to advance in a single file.

"We're in dire need of more resources and assistance," said Dr Eghbal, his voice echoing the collective concern.

Immediately, one individual was dispatched to contact the city authorities. He soon returned with the head of the gendarmerie, his assistant, and the mayor. The top officer's assurance of their support provided us with a moment of relief.

"In thirty minutes, I will return with more cars for your transportation," he said. "The mayor and I will try to arrange a contingent to intercept the wounded on the other side of the river." We eagerly awaited their return.

As he was leaving, we asked him about the city's resistance and the status of the siege.

"They have to go over my dead body before capturing the city," the officer replied.

Our rations had dwindled drastically; we were tired and hungry. Unbeknownst to us, during the chaos, the hospital's radiologist, a few doctors, and other aides abandoned their posts and ran away. Once the authorities left to organize the transport of the wounded, we mobilized all the remaining personnel and anxiously waited to hear from the mayor's office and the gendarmerie. In the meantime, the relentless bombardment continued.

"It's way past the thirty minutes we were promised," someone said frustratedly.

Two people were sent to investigate. Fifteen minutes later, we saw them coming back, looking dejected.

"The top officer and the mayor are nowhere to be found."

Panic set in. Many were terrified and nervous. Some broke down.

Dr Eghbal announced, "Everyone is on their own! I am no longer able to decide for others."

Fear filled the hallways. Our chances of breaking through the tightening circle were diminishing by the minute. For some of us, being captured was the last and worst option. If I had to choose between action and inaction, irrespective of its consequences, I would side with the former. We could take advantage of our meagre chance and maybe come out alive.

As the seconds ticked by, the silence in the room was deafening. No one had any suggestions, and our options were rapidly dwindling.

"We are going to the river!" I yelled. "Place the severely injured in the ambulances! Everyone who can walk will follow the convoy! No one can bring any of their belongings! We will all go together in a single file!"

Astonishingly, this was precisely what each person wanted to hear. Without delay, the ambulances filled with the severely injured. Behind the ambulances, less critically wounded people were assisted by someone healthier. At the back of the column were people who could manage by themselves.

I chose to sit in the first ambulance beside the driver, who knew the way to the river. Our only protection was an armed *Basijee*, a member of the volunteer branch of the Islamic Revolutionary Guard Corps, who was assigned to the hospital. He sat by the window on the passenger side.

As we were leaving, I went to the back of the convoy to ensure everyone was ready. Suddenly, I noticed that the man who had accompanied Nima and me from the factory and had impersonated a nurse a day ago was slipping his bag into one of the vehicles. I grabbed the bag and hurled it as far as possible into the yard. It's incredible how one gains more strength during exceptional moments.

"Do you value your bag more than the injured?" I shouted in front of everyone.

He remained silent. I thought of his selfishness and Dr Eghbal's loss of nerve. I wondered why people crumble in critical moments. Many cannot relinquish their self-serving traits, and others can't carry their weight. Yet, in contrast, some are willing to do more. What are the driving forces that compel people to react differently? When confronted with exceptional situations, could people's behaviour be significantly affected by their lifetime exposure to various circumstances and events, norms, mores, sufferings, social relations and structures, and social status?

The sounds of heavy machine-gun fire, the thunder of tank and artillery shells, all indicated that Iraqi ground troops were closing in. By a stroke of luck, the timing of our departure was to our advantage. The final attack was anticipated sometime near daybreak, so moving before sunrise gave us a better chance to break the siege.

Before entering the first ambulance, I glanced again at our hastily assembled caravan. All the wounded were somehow accounted for, and everyone was ready for departure. Very little time elapsed between our decision to act and our push toward the river. The drivers were directed to turn off their headlights, so in semi-darkness, we navigated a narrow dirt road by moonlight. Every time we negotiated a turn, the anticipation of Iraqi soldiers suddenly emerging before us was agonizing. I could feel my heart beating in my chest.

As we advanced, we tried our utmost to be as silent as possible, but the branches scraped the side of our vehicles, and the potholes were too many to avoid. Each time we hit a bump, I cringed at the pain the injured had to endure. Maybe hope acted as an opiate to partially curtail their agony. I had to maintain a delicate balance between my deep desire to find the river and my endless concern for the people walking behind the ambulances, which led to moments of intense anxiety. Feelings of determination, eagerness, apprehension, and restlessness were acting in unison as if I had one emotion.

Surprisingly, as we approached the river, explosions and gunfire subsided. We could hear sporadic blasts of artillery shells coming from a distance, though considerably fewer compared to half an hour before. I was puzzled. Was this the prelude to the final assault? My only hope was to find enough time for all of us to cross the river. As we came to a small mound about 20 metres from the bank, we stopped our ambulance, and the whole convoy came to a standstill.

"Can you see if everything is clear?" I asked the armed Basijee.

After around thirty seconds, he returned and said, "It looks okay."

While the patients were removed from the ambulances, the Basijee and I looked for the dinghy. To our dismay, it was on the other side of the river, and the water was fast and turbulent, wide and deep.

11
The River

Courage is resistance to fear, mastery of fear – not absence of fear.
Mark Twain

On those stormy, cold, wintery days in California's Corona del Mar, the red flag was a stark warning, urging everyone to stay clear of the water. Yet, my brother at age twenty and I at eighteen, both full of youthful bravado, were undeterred. The waves were monstrous, so high and rough that they would push us and our surfboards back toward the shore. But we were drawn to the challenge, deciding to take our adventure to the next level. We made our way to the end of the pier, ready to jump into the ocean behind the breaking waves. As I caught the first wave, the water under my board disappeared, and I fell into the base of the wave, losing my board. The waves kept twisting and turning me, making it a daunting task to find a way to the sea surface. In that moment of panic, I suddenly found myself touching the bottom of the ocean. When I changed direction and swam up, I saw the light in the distance but was almost entirely out of air. Despite enduring the fury of a few other waves, I managed to get behind them; however, the current moved me away from the shore. To escape the intensity of the riptide, I knew that swimming parallel to the shoreline might be a way out.

With a steady pace, for a long stretch, I swam relentlessly until the riptide faded. As I reached the shore, my body was utterly exhausted. My brother lay on the sand a little further away. The sight of him brought a great deal of relief but also a stark realization of how close we had come to dying. Our swimming skills had been our lifeline, saving us from the ocean's wrath.

The Basijee's voice instantly snapped me out of my reverie. "Who among you is swimming to the other side?"

"Don't worry," I said, my voice filled with determination. "I will."

The current was fierce, making a direct swim to the dinghy impossible. To reach its vicinity, I had to move upstream about 300 metres before jumping into the water. Two others, who also knew how to swim, followed me. As soon as we reached the other side of the river, I grabbed the dinghy. But while I turned to ask for help from the other two, I was met with a shocking sight. They were on the bank, running away to save themselves. I was stunned by their actions. Nevertheless, I turned the dinghy, sat inside, and pulled along the rope.

Heavy mortar, tank, and artillery shells began to rain on the river. It appeared that the final attack had commenced. Suddenly, in the middle of the river, a strange thought came to me: what if a few in our convoy panicked and rushed toward me? The dinghy could sink, and then all would be lost. I decided to bluff my way out of this difficulty, hoping to deter any potential panic.

"Stand on high ground and shoot anyone who rushes the dinghy," I shouted to the Basijee.

Then I was consumed by worry: What if he shoots someone? Would I ever forgive myself? But at that moment, I knew I had to take the risk. The responsibility was mine to bear.

Upon reaching the shore, the seriously injured were mostly paired with healthier individuals, so assistance was available on the other side. Despite the unrelenting onslaught of explosions, we didn't hesitate on our first trip. After reaching the far shore, the injured were evacuated. I went back for more wounded as the sound of machine gunfire intensified in the distance.

On the third trip, an artillery shell hit the water while those less injured and I pulled the rope. I was seated facing an older man from a nearby village. The tip of my boots touched the front portion of his worn slippers. Suddenly, a piece of shrapnel hit the top of his left foot; blood gushed out into the boat and over my boots. A man beside him placed a handkerchief on the wound and pressed hard. We were 4 metres from the far shore. To prevent further bleeding, he tied the two ends of the cloth firmly around the older man's foot and helped him to disembark. Now that the seriously injured were evacuated, unsurprisingly, not even one person offered to stay on the return trip.

As I continued pulling the rope to reach the injured for the next trip, I looked to my right, about 10 metres further ahead, and noticed a man in the water. His presence added a new layer of complexity to an already dire situation. I couldn't tell if he was swimming or struggling to stay afloat. At that moment, I felt the weight of responsibility on my shoulders. Should I abandon the injured and rush to his aid, or should I continue with the mission? The decision was mine to make. If I chose to save him, I had no assurance of anyone bringing the dinghy back.

Although one rarely encounters situations of this magnitude, it's a life-changing choice when it happens. To comfort ourselves, maybe we unconsciously try to rationalize and think optimistically. Momentarily, I had satisfied myself that he wouldn't drown. Therefore, my decision was not to leave the injured. Yet, even now, the uncertainty of his survival lingers.

We lived through explosions and made seven trips, transporting more than fifty individuals. On our sixth trip, Nima was paired with an injured man to help him on the other side. At this time, we could hear the sound of gunfire not too far away. When the final run came around, it was time for the Basijee to join us, having stood steadfast at his post. His unwavering determination, a source of inspiration, increased my admiration. Even though our viewpoints were extremely far apart, we were drawn together through our actions.

"Please, search the area and make certain that no one was left behind," I shouted before asking him to come aboard.

"Everyone has apparently gone to the other side," he said, looking around.

Hearing this assurance, I felt more convinced that others in our convoy had swum to safety while transporting people.

On our last trip, as we rapidly pulled the rope, a mortar shell hit the wooden post on the side we were approaching. The rope went slack and fell into the water. Astonishingly, not even one piece of shrapnel hit our boat. We were only a few metres from the shore; everyone began paddling with their hands, and we soon collided with the bank.

At this time, we were facing the peak of the Iraqi army's attack. When I looked away from the river toward where we needed to go, all I could see was a long stretch of barren land. However, barely visible in the distance, I could make out a mountain range. As we prepared for the journey, I came across a mother and a daughter who needed help. The daughter, who was about fourteen years old, had one stump foot, which impeded her ability to walk. To make matters worse, even in those harsh circumstances, she contended with a black veil that she chose to tie around her waist rather than discard. Considering the great distance before us, I decided to carry her on my back.

As we began our march, I heard several whizzing noises and countless explosions. The whizzing sounds differed from the regular machine-gun bullets, and it didn't take long before I realized their source. About 5 metres away, a young man fell to the ground. I set the girl down and went to check on him. He had been hit by an anti-aircraft bullet, which had entered his back, likely piercing his heart and chest. He had died instantly. It seemed that the Iraqi army had noticed many people trying to escape and was firing anti-aircraft bullets randomly at ground level to cause as much damage as possible. As we tried to figure out what to do, the frequency of the whizzing sounds increased. With great reluctance, we left the body and continued to move away from the river.

We travelled for hours, and the weight of the young girl on my back was a constant reminder of our perilous situation. The scorching, barren land seemed to stretch on endlessly. In such circumstances, the mind becomes solely occupied with survival, and a surge of energy invigorates the body. All trivial matters are entirely forgotten. In some ways, one focuses only on factors that protect and preserve. The last time I drank water was a few hours before leaving the hospital, yet I was completely unaware of my thirst in those harsh conditions. When I left the river, my boots were heavy and soaking wet. Yet, after our long walk, I noticed they were completely dry. Not once had I noticed their slushiness or became annoyed by their weight.

After some time, we noticed several army vehicles close to the mountains. As we drew near, it became certain that we had reached safety. We were greeted by a few soldiers who immediately offered their assistance. We shook their hands and embraced one another with great exhilaration and relief. They took us to a shaded area to rest and quench our thirst, and after a few minutes, they began to arrange our transportation to Ahvaz.

Somehow, I had the urge to stay in the area. I wasn't sure why, but I was restless and uneasy. In some way, I felt responsible, knowing that by default, I had assumed the leadership of our convoy. At that moment, I thought: what if, after crossing the river, some wounded were unwittingly left behind? A profound feeling of guilt and obligation overwhelmed me. I had to act. I went to an officer and asked him if he could take me to the river in his Jeep – at that time, the army was separate from the Revolutionary Guard Corps or its affiliate, the *Basij*. To my surprise, he agreed and called another soldier to accompany us. The three of us headed back.

We drove the same route I had painfully crossed a few hours earlier. The hot desert wind battered our faces vigorously, feeling like a relentless flogging. Despite the challenging conditions, our eagerness to not leave anyone behind compelled us to continue. We had no choice but to assume that the Iraqi army had not crossed the water. As we got to within 200 metres of the river, a barrage of machine-gun fire came toward us, causing the driver of the Jeep to panic and drive into a ditch. We jumped out and lay low for a few seconds. Then, to find better cover, we crawled on our bellies until we reached a mud hut.

We were about 50 metres from where I had abandoned the dinghy earlier that morning, though it felt like I'd done that days ago. After surveying the area and finding no sign of any injured person from our convoy, I set out to find the source of the gunfire. Carefully scanning the area from the corner of the hut to the other side of the river, I spotted the heads of Iraqi soldiers on the prowl for us.

We crawled out of their range for a long distance. Then, bent over for some time, we passed our wrecked Jeep. After many arduous hours, just before sunset, we were back at the camp. The physical toll of the journey was evident in our exhausted bodies. Fortunately, they had a helicopter available, which took us to Ahvaz.

Upon my arrival, I met with my colleagues from the factory. We proceeded to the nearby hospital and visited the injured from our convoy. We were warmly greeted. While others shared their experiences and encounters with danger, I discreetly took a head count. Once I ascertained that most had made it to Ahvaz, I felt a sense of relief.

As I left our quarters early the following day to check in on the patients again, I was unprepared for what I was about to experience. Approaching the hospital entrance, I was taken aback to see the same Basijee who had assisted us during the river incident. His reaction on seeing me was unexpected. He came toward me and, to my surprise, kissed my forehead.

"I don't care what your beliefs are. I can only say that I wish more of your kind were on our side," he said, his words carrying a weight of appreciation that transcended our differences.

"Your bravery was admirable!" I replied. "I'm glad you were assigned to assist us."

"Your actions have altered my perceptions about your kind," he stated, acknowledging my secular beliefs.

"Perhaps a day will come when you and I can climb the same mountain from two different sides, reach the summit, and find less suffering," I responded.

His impulsive gesture sent me into a reflective state. Why did I take the lead by default? Did I need to prove something to myself or others? Was my behaviour purely altruistic? I had no explanation. I only knew that his fair-mindedness had urged me to think. I also recognized that his reaction spawned in me a feeling of humility. I realized that his honesty generated mutual respect regardless of our dissimilar viewpoints. Before speaking, he must have challenged his internal biases, which should be considered courageous. At that juncture, he had reached levels of empowerment that the less authentic could never comprehend. The Basijees were a heterogeneous organization mainly recruited from the lower socio-economic stratum. They were propagandized to think negatively of the secular left; however, a few ventured out and showed some independence.

As I left him and entered the hospital, a staff member rushed out, his face beaming with joy. He shouted, "The siege of Susangerd is broken! The city is free from occupation!" His words echoed with relief.

Despite the joy, a cloud of concern loomed over me as I pondered the hospital's condition. I couldn't shake off the worry that it might have been demolished by bombardment or vandalized by the Iraqi army. The thought of its plight lingered in my mind. It's remarkable how investing time, effort, and sweat in a place inevitably leads to a profound sense of attachment. After discussing it with friends, I was convinced I could be more helpful in Susangerd.

So, early the next day, I found an army truck heading that way.

12

Susangerd

Courage is grace under pressure.
Ernest Hemingway

The driver, a soldier who shuttled food supplies, was a chubby, talkative man with a long moustache covering half his mouth. His chatter was incessant, jumping from one topic to another and asking many questions. As I struggled to keep up with his conversation, my mind wandered to the scenery and the road. I couldn't help but recall my first experience travelling the same route some days ago. Yet, this trip felt radically different from the first, as if I had been transported to another time and place with a completely different atmosphere. Can one's perception of the same surroundings change after witnessing unimaginable events? Like a flip side of déjà vu? Nevertheless, when we approached the outskirts of Susangerd, I noticed that the countryside had been drastically altered. It was heart-breaking to see the massive devastation of the city and its surroundings – the ravages of war had exposed the ugly side of humankind.

When we reached the hospital, fortunately, most of the main building stood tall against the backdrop of destruction. Stepping through the central door, I confronted a scene of abandonment and lifelessness. A small area on the hospital's south side appeared as I walked through the main hallway. It was cordoned off for emergency medical use. Staff members, unfamiliar to me, were gathered in one corner. I introduced myself as a volunteer, and the head nurse swiftly briefed me on my duties. A few minutes later, as I headed to the main lobby to look for my belongings, I was relieved to find my sleeping bag and small carry-on case unharmed, a minor success in the face of disaster.

Later that day, I stepped outside for a brief break. The sight of the destruction was staggering. As I approached the main street, I spotted a few soldiers carrying a wounded man. I joined them, and together, we made our way to the hospital. After handing over the injured man to a nurse, I noticed a change in the soldiers' attitude. They seemed to be aware of the river episode and were more co-operative and respectful than they might have been.

Mid-morning the next day, two soldiers entered the hospital and called out my name. As I approached them, a man armed with a Kalashnikov stepped forward.

"You need to come with us now. It's urgent," one of the soldiers said with a serious tone.

Why would they send for me? My mind raced with this and other questions. After navigating through the city streets and some alleys, we arrived at the front door of a building; the purpose of our journey was still a puzzle to me.

"Get in!" one of them said.

At their headquarters, their senior officer explained why I was summoned.

"There is a dried-up river on the west side of the city. The Iraqis are on the other side, and we have held our ground on this side. As of this moment, there hasn't been any movement. It appears that we are temporarily at an impasse. No one dares to cross the bridge."

"Why do you need me?" I inquired.

"On their side, below the bridge, there is a drop where the Iraqis have no visibility," he explained solemnly. "As we were retreating to this side, one of our men got trapped. Now that the Iraqis are secured in their positions, he cannot come to our side without exposing himself to their sharpshooters. We've heard of your previous efforts and think maybe you can find a way to get him out of this predicament."

I was startled by their level of confidence in me. Then, I realized this was part of why I had become a volunteer. I was determined to demonstrate that secular volunteers could make a difference and show leadership, no matter the circumstances.

The two of us moved quickly through more streets and alleys of Susangerd. When we approached the bridge, I noticed several soldiers behind barricades, inside huts and ditches. The atmosphere was tense, and the anticipation of an imminent attack was palpable, hanging heavy in the air.

The person who briefed me spoke with a hint of composure, but his body language betrayed his fear. As I crawled toward the bridge, I spotted a young man in a small ditch, a pile of dirt in front of him for protection. His main task was monitoring the activities on the other side, but even his confident exterior couldn't conceal the fear in his eyes.

"How many times have their sharpshooters fired at you this morning?" I asked the young man.

"A few times an hour. I try not to unduly expose myself while keeping an eye on them," the young man replied, his voice steady and resolute despite the constant threat.

"You have an important job," I said. "Be careful." From his vantage point, I saw a young man in his teens curled up close to the side pylon on the other side below the bridge. His thighs were touching his chest, and both arms clutched his legs. Above him was a metal bridge supported with trusses above and below. The formation of the trusses in the lower part of the bridge was such that one could easily walk on its I-beams and cross the river without taking the usual way across the bridge.

It was a critical moment. I had to summon all my courage. Life seldom presents us with occasions when one is truly tested. Yet, even in those moments, fear is a relentless companion. As I returned to the previous barricade, I repeatedly reminded myself, *You can't escape fear; you must manage it*. But somehow, this greater-than-self cause ignited a fire within me, giving me the strength to move forward.

Next, I asked to see the person in charge of the group. A tall man with broad shoulders stepped forward. He had a rifle in one hand and a map of the area in the other. After surveying the buildings in the vicinity, I told him that I would go underneath the bridge, move inside the lower trusses, walk on top of the I-beams, and try to return on the same path with the trapped man.

"The only caveat," I told him, "is that before I'm exposed to their line of fire, your men must ceaselessly fire at the other side. Hopefully, the sheer volume of firepower will force them to take cover, which might impede their chances of firing back. During this crucial period, your men must continue firing to their last bullet."

He became very emotional, a testament to the gravity of the situation.

"We will not let you down, and until both of you are safe, we will fire in their direction non-stop," he said, as his nostrils flared.

"Thank you for understanding the situation," I acknowledged, reiterating the importance of the plan. I then instructed everyone to start firing when I brought my hand down.

Before executing the plan, I experienced a surge of adrenalin. My mind sharpened by focusing on the present, and fear momentarily vanished. Remarkably, my body was primed. Around noon, I signalled to all the soldiers to open fire at will. As the bullets struck the buildings on the other side, I sprinted as fast as I could. In a few heartbeats, I reached the side pylon of the bridge, leapt onto the lower truss, and moved swiftly along the I-beams. I grabbed the trapped man's hand and retraced my steps. Bullets were raining down around us. I couldn't discern if all the firing was coming from our side. When we reached the end of the lower truss, I pushed him up from the side of the bridge to the top of the pylon. I positioned myself behind him, and we both dashed toward safety.

After we reached one of the barricades, all gunfire from our side instantly stopped. It seemed that the barrage had paralyzed the other side. The whole episode lasted about three minutes. I glanced at the formerly trapped man's face. He looked like a child who had just escaped a lion's den; simultaneously, he radiated exhilaration and gratitude. However, before we could celebrate his rescue, a mortar shell hit the ditch where I had earlier spoken to the young man watching the other side. I rushed to help, but the largest body part I could see was around the size of a softball. Tears blurred my vision; he was young, confident, full of hope, and proud of being the first to alert his group of the Iraqi attack. His death was one of many tragedies.

As I returned to the hospital around 2 p.m., the weight of what had just transpired hung heavy in the air. The loss of that young man, the thought of his life fading into insignificance, and the grim reality of such brutality becoming normalized in war – all these emotions weighed heavily on my heart. Perhaps one of the greatest tragedies we face is accepting such incidents as a regular part of life in war.

Eventually, I decided to rest. I must have dozed off when a soldier came in with disturbing news.

"The Iraqi army has encircled us for the second time."

After all I had gone through, hearing the news of the second encirclement was like a physical blow. The stress of the situation was heavy on my already burdened shoulders. Yet, I knew I had to gather enough resilience to accept what had happened and find a way out.

I stayed in the hospital, bracing myself for a rush of new wounded. We all clung to the hope of a counterattack that would break the siege. And our expectation was fulfilled: the counteroffensive arrived in a relatively short period, freeing us from the looming threat of capture or worse. The relief was immediate, and the joy of our rescue was a euphoric wave that overwhelmed us.

At around 6 p.m., I arrived in Ahvaz and met my colleagues from the factory.

"While you were in Susangerd, the authorities became suspicious and were looking for you," Nima informed me. "They detained me for one night."

I was horrified to hear the news. He was interrogated for many hours. Their investigation revolved around why we had come to the front lines and my whereabouts. For the moment, they accepted Nima's explanation. However, due to the presence of many autonomous centres of power, there was a great possibility of being summoned again. Although the authorities had asked for volunteers from the beginning of the war, they pushed the narrative that only religious forces were involved. They didn't want secular people like us to change their narrative and be active in the war zone. It wasn't safe to stay in the region any longer. The potential of being detained by the same people who apprehended Nima, or other authorities, increased by the hour. We decided to return to the factory immediately. The next afternoon, two vehicles arrived to take us home.

I walked into my apartment; all I could think about was a long sleep, which wasn't possible. Early the next morning, we were all back at our departments. A few days later, I was astonished to learn that a newspaper was interested in parts of our experience. Even more surprising was that our story was published and circulated within just a few weeks. Most of the article quoted me; this is my translation in English of two separate excerpts (shown in figures 12.1 and 12.2):

> The hospital was filled with injured patients, some waiting for surgery and others recuperating. Meanwhile, the wounded were being admitted in a continual progression. However, we couldn't transport the injured due to the roadblock to Ahvaz and the city's siege. Additionally, the uninterrupted explosions from mortar shells created a tense atmosphere in the hospital. Consequently, the supervisor of the radiology department, along with a few doctors, nurses, and volunteers, left the hospital. A mortar shell hit the engine room. The hospital became dark. Surgery ceased, putting the injured at risk.

> While feeling a lump in my throat, I cried out in a cracked voice: "Why doesn't anyone decide or do something? Get the ambulances ready! We need to evacuate all the wounded! Not a single injured person should remain!" Instantly, the silence gripping the hospital broke. Once again, while feeling the lump in my throat, I shouted,

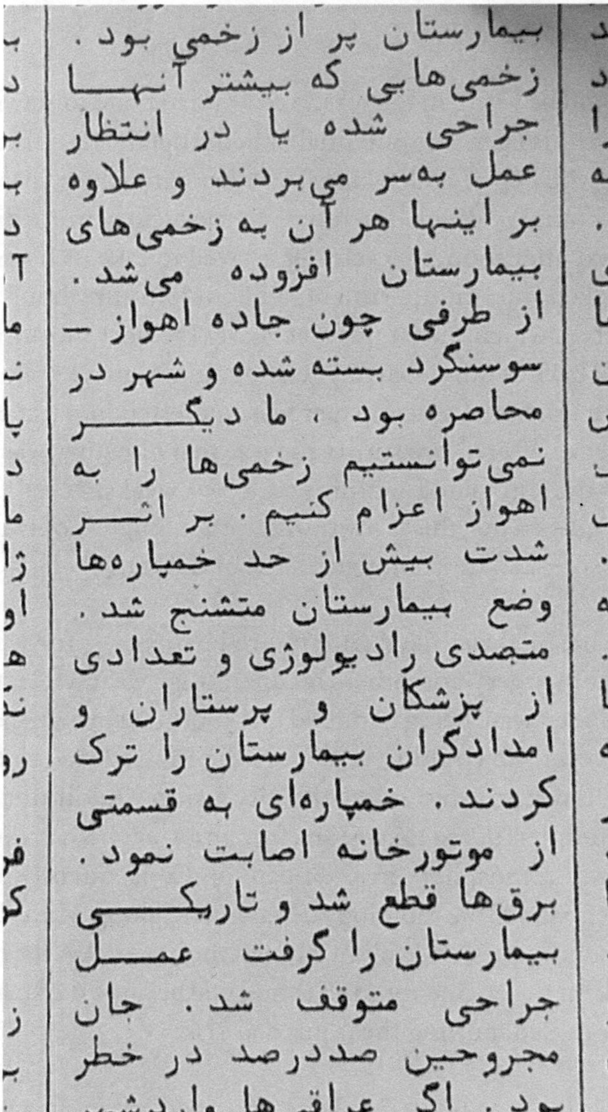

بیمارستان پر از زخمی بود.
زخمی‌هایی که بیشتر آنها
جراحی شده یا در انتظار
عمل به‌سر می‌بردند و علاوه
بر اینها هر آن به زخمی‌های
بیمارستان افزوده می‌شد.
از طرفی چون جاده اهواز ـ
سوسنگرد بسته شده و شهر در
محاصره بود، ما دیگر
نمی‌توانستیم زخمی‌ها را به
اهواز اعزام کنیم. بر اثر
شدت بیش از حد خمپاره‌ها
وضع بیمارستان متشنج شد.
متصدی رادیولوژی و تعدادی
از پزشکان و پرستاران و
امدادگران بیمارستان را ترک
کردند. خمپاره‌ای به قسمتی
از موتورخانه اصابت نمود.
برق‌ها قطع شد و تاریکی
بیمارستان را گرفت عمل
جراحی متوقف شد. جان
مجروحین صددرصد در خطر
بود. اگر عراقی‌ها وارد شهر

Figures 12.1 *above* and 12.2 *opposite*
From a newspaper article, two separate excerpts describe a chaotic moment during the siege at Susangerd Hospital. The full article highlights the nuances of human behaviour when confronted with near-death experiences, illustrating how some individuals respond responsibly while others do not.

با صدای بغض‌آلود و گرفته‌ای فریاد زدم :

" پس چرا تصمیمی نمی‌گیرید ؟ ! . . . چرا کاری نمی‌کنید ؟ ! . . . آمبولانس‌ها را آماده کنید . . . همه زخمی‌ها را باید بیرون ببریم . . . حتی یک زخمی هم اینجا نمی‌باید بماند . "

سکوتی که بیمارستان را گرفته بود ، شکسته شد . هنوز بغض گلویم را می‌فشرد . چند بار فریاد زدم :

" زخمی‌های بدحال را به آمبولانس‌ها منتقل کنید . . . همگی با زخمی‌هایی که می‌توانند راه بروند در یک صف حرکت خواهیم کرد . "

جنب و جوشی بیمارستان را گرفت . همه دست به کار شدیم . آمبولانس‌ها را تا آنجا که جا داشتند ، از زخمی‌های بدحال پر کردیم .

"Place the severely injured in the ambulances first! The rest will follow in line with those who can walk!" My command sparked a flurry of activity in the hospital, and all the seriously injured were loaded into ambulances.

13
Reflection

I feel at home in the entire world, wherever there are clouds and birds and human tears.
Rosa Luxemburg

The first few workdays back at the factory were tough, but I found the strength to push through. I had witnessed unimaginable scenes, and my attempts to brush aside the thoughts of countless sufferings became useless, which, in due course, took its toll. Yet, life continued, and time – the great healer – softened the pain. Still, I wondered if total healing was possible. Maybe time partly repairs the affliction, but the residual effects can endure.

Finally, I found some normalcy by immersing myself in work: projects like statistical analysis, organizational review, and optimization assignments, as well as many hours on tasks that involved people. This process allowed me to gain a deeper understanding of my colleagues' needs. As a result, some of them became more receptive, collaborative, and less hesitant as time passed. Eventually, I was able to enjoy friendly relationships with numerous people.

At this point, having worked in the United States and, to a lesser extent, in Iran, I became interested in comparing the cultural attitudes toward work in both societies. Reflecting on my various jobs in California, some very demanding and others less so, I found that in North American society, the lower and middle classes generally value work, regardless of its nature. On the other hand, in cultures like Iran, which hold more traces of feudal tradition, the upper and middle classes tend to be more selective about their jobs. The middle class may not accept any position unless compelled to move down the social ladder.

This positive attitude toward work in some sectors of North America may have been influenced by the onset of modernity after the Industrial Revolution in Europe, as well as the need for the North American pioneers to survive at any cost. However, it's important not to overlook the dark history associated with the pioneers' settler-colonial project. They pillaged and ravaged the Indigenous Peoples, destroying their culture and habitat. The pioneers' exploits teem with atrocities. Moreover, the tragic and violent history of slavery further intensified these horrifying abuses. Yet, over time, they learned more deceptive and sophisticated ways of dominance, using more nuanced forms of control.

Based on my field of study and exposure to different production processes, I've realized that work experience can significantly contribute to driving innovation, provided that other demands don't overshadow the self-satisfaction that comes from creating. This feeling of fulfillment is a crucial component of the creative process. For instance, assembly-line workers focus solely on their specific task, often missing out on the joy of witnessing the final product that eventually results from the efforts of many hands. While this method can improve efficiency, it may also hinder creativity. Nonetheless, in today's hectic world, for many hard-working individuals, the urgency of providing for their family often takes precedence over finding fulfillment in their work and enjoying the impact of their creations. Instead of work being a source of dignity, status, self-worth, security, and a meaningful role in society, most people simply exchange labour for wages. The balance between work and leisure time also becomes skewed, leading to an increase in chronic stress.

Thereby, those in positions of power can take advantage of people's positive attitudes toward work, leaving little time to genuinely sit back and reflect. Consequently, conformity persists and a few benefit disproportionately from the hard work of many.

When comparing the Iranian and US top-down organizational relationships of the factories I worked at, I noticed differences and similarities. One significant parallel was the ability of the top of the pyramid to control the flow of information in their favour. The most important difference in post-revolution Iran was that the top of the organizational pyramid had two heads. One was the management, and the other was the Islamic Association. The latter was a branch affiliated with the government and connected to its mother organization outside of the factory. Their informal authority generated a great deal of influence, significantly impacting the power dynamics and the function of management, relegating them to a ceremonial role and to mainly carrying out technical or administrative tasks.

Also, my experiences living in the United States and later in Iran prompted me to explore the contrast between various societal structures. While some might argue that "open societies" already exist in the West, I became increasingly disillusioned as I examined the true nature of these societies. It became clear to me that the government, instead of being "by the people and for the people," is heavily influenced by corporations. Many projects do not benefit the public. People often feel disempowered. The masses tend to be held back and lack enlightened thinking. While I recognized that counterclaims might be valid in some circumstances, I found it essential to resolve a crucial question for myself: what is the difference between an authentic open society – one that serves all its people and treats its less fortunate with some degree of fairness – and a less authentic open society, such as those found in most Western countries, as well as an authoritarian society. My primary focus was to understand the form of accountability that those at the top of the social pyramid must deliver to those at the base.

I became very interested in the works of many progressive political philosophers. Each extensively elaborates on how individuals in so-called open societies are subtly manipulated into passivity and conformity. Through the work of these intellectuals, I realized how a fabricated culture of consumption and immediate pleasures creates a false psychological need for material goods and services. In their works, I found many ways in which mass media and other institutions constantly bombard people with messages that entice them into buying, irrespective of their economic status. This false psychological need can overshadow authentic happiness, real freedom, innate creativity, and artistic imagination.

Furthermore, their work compelled me to consider how mass media, often with the covert but significant support of corporations and governments, acts as a potent ideological institution that serves the interests of the powerful. Noam Chomsky's "manufacturing consent" system is a chilling revelation of how people can be led to believe they have a choice even when they do not, whether in their purchasing decisions, voting, or thinking a certain way. Unbeknownst to them, they have been subjected to a propaganda communication model. They internalize certain assumptions and fall into self-censorship without overt coercion.

This persuasion method employed by various mass media in the West, particularly those predominantly promoting the narrative of the Establishment, alarmed me. I found two of their approaches especially effective. The first technique is to report events selectively. When multiple newsworthy stories are available, most mainstream journalists cover the ones that fit their narrative and ignore others. I realized that overlooking newsworthy events can be more effective than reporting their chosen events. I became convinced that the power to decide what to report and what not to report is crucial in pursuing their vision, and the irony lies in the Establishment's claim that reporters are impartial. Their assertion that they separate commentary or opinions from news seemed merely a manoeuvre.

I noticed that this technique relies heavily on loaded terminologies that support the Establishment's narrative. It's difficult to erase a first impression planted in the minds of readers or listeners; words like "pro-democracy," "anti-authoritarian," or "backed by" have a significant psychological impact. When mainstream journalists, whether consciously or unconsciously, fail to use neutral language when reporting on demonstrations or movements, they are not just reporting but also expressing their opinions, distorting the objective nature of the news.

The second strategy that caught my attention was how these reporters inundated and misled the public with half-truths. This approach can be more potent than false statements, as it can be easier to defend and tougher for the opposition to discredit. I witnessed many cases in which a narrative requiring more evidence was reported without offering an opposing viewpoint, especially if the news involved a rival country. Other like-minded reporters would then circulate the same perspective. Over time, this story became accepted as "fact" by many media outlets and their audiences or readers. Furthermore, obscure or biased "experts" – some from unknown or dubious think-tanks – would occasionally be invited on radio, TV, and other platforms to discuss these matters without a vetting process to determine their credibility.

I became convinced that echoing the Establishment's narrative doesn't necessarily need to involve the head of a particular media company (although, if true, this is usually disputed by many as a "conspiracy theory"). Countless reporters realize a relationship exists between their job's security or promotion and their performance in toeing the accepted lines. For many, their financial pressures often force making a living more pressing than their moral obligation. Sadly, reporters who withstand the pressure and stick to their principles don't usually have long tenures.

A few questions troubled me the most. Is it possible for the mass media to be unbiased when powerful corporations own it? Is impartiality possible when ad revenues are on the line? Can one believe the claim that there is an arm's-length relationship between the owners and the journalists when profit is paramount? How can this separation be controlled? Is conflict of interest conveniently ignored?

In my readings, I discovered that Western governmental and non-governmental institutions use various control techniques to bring elements of the population into conformity. Different power relationships not only manage people's behaviour in terms of hierarchical, top-down control, typically exerted by the state, but also as a form of internalized perception imposed upon individuals from different levels of civil society and the family.

Social control also emanates from institutions such as the film industry, theatre performances, professional associations, media, schools, medical centres, mental health facilities, prisons, and more. However, it's encouraging to note that, as a rule, an intricate form of resistance usually emerges from the bottom-up to counter these control techniques.

In devouring the books of progressive political philosophers, I became fascinated with their explanation of why, in the less authentic open societies of the West, individuals can become alienated from their family, work, community, and environment. I was surprised by how people can become apathetic toward politics, life, and the future.

Every four years, the United States presidential elections turn into a high-stakes horse race, as depicted by the mass media and various interest groups. This creates an environment where voters face a limited choice between two parties. Significant barriers are devised to prevent the rise of a viable third party that isn't tied to the Establishment's narrative. As a result, voters often feel trapped in a two-party system that fails to represent their interests. Many unwittingly become part of this game, oblivious to the fact that instead of engaging in a credible democratic process, they are lured into a contest that often serves to settle disputes between factions in power. And yet, in a rare case, when someone not entirely beholden to the Establishment comes along, the mass media and the powerful join hands to discredit their candidacy. Sadly, many voters have become accustomed to the spread of disinformation by the elite and the media. They erroneously associate new ideas that could help their plight with mere ploys to make them pay more taxes.

And so, the most outstanding achievement of many less authentic open societies and totalitarian regimes is the ability of the state and other institutions to create resourceful distractions. These diversionary tactics can generate compliance and apathy. Equally, I wondered if the indifference cultivated toward politics may partly be a strategy to curtail activists' challenge to authority.

I was intrigued by how authorities create a culture of fear in times of crisis. It became evident that they frequently use the threat of "others" to support their narrative. They often fabricate events or exploit emerging incidents to perpetuate this practice. As a result, security becomes a top priority. Psychologically, portraying others as fundamentally different from us – depicting them as evil and alien to our way of life – dehumanizes them, making them easier to reject. However, if we unexpectedly come into contact with these others, we may find our commonalities, sparking a connection.

It became clear to me that the Establishment's cultural dominance imposes certain values as normal, causing us to internalize their standards and accept them as our own. In contrast, over many years of struggle and continuous pressure from the disaffected base of society, people in these less authentic open societies have gained rights and civil liberties that are not comparable to those in harsh totalitarian regimes. These rights and freedoms are not granted from above; rather, they are only achieved through the collective efforts arising from the bottom-up pressure.

What's particularly striking about these less authentic open societies is the contrast they present. Instead of displaying the crude and callous responses typical of authoritarian countries, they exhibit a subtle form of manipulation – what Freddie Mercury referred to as "cool deception" in his song "Heaven for Everyone."

He argues that the world can be where everyone is fed and has fun, with "heaven for everyone." In this "world of cool deception," he passionately advocates for love instead of rejection and discusses what is done to people's souls. Ultimately, he condemns the taking of lives, the destruction of aspirations, and the stripping away of a person's pride and dignity without a shred of compassion.

I often wonder about the widespread apathy in North America. Is it conceivable that, whether consciously or unconsciously, we are losing our vital social connection due to our disengagement? Have we grown indifferent to the suffering of others around the world? Are we reaching a point in our daily lives where we turn a blind eye to discrimination, intolerance, abuse, and cruelty? I have come to believe that the exploited suffer so profoundly that it ultimately deprives them of the life we all deserve.

Moreover, the mass media often acts as a tool for the abusers, downplaying and normalizing such behaviour. If we continue on this path, will we become acclimated, complacent, and unable to empathize? What is the connection between affluence and having a spectator mentality? Can the worship of privilege make us more susceptible to insensitivity? From my experiences, I am uncertain whether the spectator is any less culpable than the abuser.

Upon completing my university education in the United States, I found myself contemplating whether we had already tipped past the precipice of an inevitable shift to a new paradigm, perhaps due to the prevailing ethos of consumerism and the material conditions humanity imposes on one another. Can we change our mindset from an unconstrained competition structure to interdependence and co-operation? Could we aspire to build a wisdom-oriented community rather than perpetuate a profit-driven society that expands at all costs?

Can pressure from the base of society be the critical agent of change? Could the quintessential achievement of any social movement be a gradual buildup of people's interest in political transformation? Can we tear down the walls of apathy by rejuvenating our capacity to overcome many inculcated fears?

I realized there comes a stage in life when we reach a crossroads and have no alternative but to opt for one of the paths. What directs us is typically predicated on our social condition, experiences, struggles in life, instincts, and the frequency of our exposure to various exceptional encounters – such as living in different environments, war, imprisonment, and the like. These experiences, I came to believe, empower us to select a path and determine our way of life. It's a choice between a fantasy world or reality.

14
Marriage

Love is an ideal thing, marriage a real thing.
Wolfgang Goethe

One day, Nima said, "I'm sure you know there is a big debate on TV tomorrow afternoon."

"Yes, it's between the representatives of the government and two leftist groups."

"Why don't we go to my sister's place and watch it?" he said.

"Why your sister's?"

"I met a girl a few days ago at a friend's house that I think is right for you. She is my friend's little sister. I want to invite her, too."

"What do you mean, right for me?"

"Well! You never know! You might get to like her," Nima said, shrugging.

"This subject hasn't been my top priority in these times."

"It's just an idea! You have nothing to lose."

After an awkward pause, I decided to step out of my comfort zone and accepted his invitation.

"I'll be there half an hour before the debate."

Nima was a good friend, a genuinely caring man whose concern about my future was apparent. Equally, I was deeply moved by his own troubles. Some years before, while studying overseas, he had married an American girl and had fathered a daughter. He also had a second daughter from his wife's first marriage. After the revolution, his wife joined him in Iran, but the post-revolutionary atmosphere overwhelmed her to the point where she took both children and left. In their correspondence, she implored him to leave Iran for the United States. He was torn between his country, with all its volatility, and his family.

The next day, I rang the bell. Nima's sister opened the door with a warm and welcoming smile, making me feel at home. Her kindness and hospitality were transparent, and I couldn't help but admire her fearlessness, knowing her war-zone story and hardships. Nima had shared with me the adversities she had faced in the last city where she had lived, enduring endless bombardment that led to her entire family's evacuation.

As I entered the apartment, Nima came forward.

"She'll be here any minute."

Just then, the bell rang. Nima's sister opened the door. Two young women walked in. Nima greeted them with a warm smile.

After introducing his sister, Nima looked toward me and said, "This is Pegah and her sister Maral."

As we sat down and started discussing the upcoming debate, it quickly became apparent that Pegah's and my viewpoints aligned. A confident and curious secular woman, she was deeply interested in current political events. Our shared interest in politics created a solid bond, and her barrage of questions only served to strengthen our connection.

As our conversation continued, I discovered she worked for an agency serving refugees in our city. Her demeanour, liveliness, and interests were appealing, and I found myself attracted but uncertain. Pegah was unaware of the agenda behind our first meeting.

After that night, I saw her three or four more times. At each meeting, we delved deeper into our shared interests. Then she invited me to meet her parents. I asked my parents to meet her in our city within three months, and shortly after that, we married.

During this period, the war raged throughout most of the country. The southwest cities were under constant bombardment. Although we weren't immune from occasional air sirens and anti-aircraft gunfire, life was generally less hectic. Every day, refugees would pour into our city and be placed anywhere unoccupied. Of course, people with means or connections would receive a better dwelling.

A few days after our marriage, Pegah asked me to come with her and meet a refugee family. At that meeting, her actions were truly inspiring. She had previously informed me of their abject poverty. As we entered a room occupied by the family, the father looked frail and coughed incessantly. He was lying on an old mattress on top of a small, dilapidated rug that was not much larger than the mattress itself. The room was bare, with no signs of comfort or luxury. He had a soiled quilt pulled up to his chest. On the other side of the room, the mother was frying a few eggplants on a kerosene stove. Their children, aged seven to sixteen, were seated on the floor alongside the wall.

As soon as we entered the room, Pegah greeted them with warmth and affection, as if we all had known one another for some time. She went to the old man, sat beside the quilt stained with food remnants, offered him his prescription drugs, and gave the mother some food coupons; life had taken its toll. Pegah's affection and lack of pretension touched me deeply, and her respectful attitude was a joy to witness. It became clear to me that despite all the hardships the family was experiencing, Pegah's approach conveyed courtesy and gave back to them the precious dignity they so rightfully desired and deserved. Her actions, though seemingly small, had a profound impact, demonstrating the transformative power of compassion in the face of adversity.

In the meantime, the news from the front fluctuated between encouraging and depressing. Both sides were gaining and losing small territories, but the front lines remained relatively stable at this point in the war.

Within a year of marriage, we were delighted to have a healthy baby boy, strengthening our relationship. However, parenthood was a growth journey, requiring us to be imaginative and work as a team. Like many new parents, we turned to how-to books for guidance, but ultimately, adapting and learning to improvise truly shaped our parenting experience.

When my boy came into this world, my life changed. It was a moment of pure joy and wonder. But sadly, I was deprived of sharing the marvel of life with Pegah – the government prohibited anyone other than the medical staff from being in the delivery room. When I was given my child to hold, the feeling of love and care was so strong that I felt something biological click in me. The three of us slept in one of the hospital rooms that first night. Pegah had the chills, so the room was sweltering – but there was nowhere else I wanted to be.

While we relished the joys of parenthood, the political unrest of the time demanded my attention. I couldn't simply ignore the erosion of civil liberties. It was a challenging balancing act that required all my determination and strength. I had to handle my social obligations alongside my responsibilities as a parent and a supportive partner.

Working at the factory took a good portion of my time. I became involved in many projects and ventures, some technical and a few others more organizational. At one point, the influential people of the factory decided to create a committee to draft a charter for establishing a *shora* (union). Most people considered the election of committee members a formality since the Islamic Association had total control over the proceedings. To this end, an assembly was arranged in the cafeteria. As soon as we arrived, the organizers asked candidates to come forward. We were to cast our votes by a show of hands. It was well known that only the association-approved candidates would step up. The association's attempt to control the proceedings was intimidating, and I felt many employees weren't represented.

To everyone's surprise, after most candidates had already stepped forward, I joined them. The organizers were clearly startled but had no choice but to allow my participation. Their next wish was for me to lose. To their complete shock and my amazement, I received the most votes.

The committee's first meeting was uncomfortable. It commenced with a prayer led by a young man who appeared very religious, a sight that immediately made me feel isolated and disconnected. The stark contrast between my beliefs and background and those of the other members was very noticeable. I didn't see the need to mix religious rituals with other social activities. So, at the start of each meeting, I discreetly tried to hide my lack of participation in their religious practices, a task that only deepened my sense of isolation.

Over time, I became known as a secular outsider.

The factory security, tied to the Islamic Association, showed interest. I was called in for what felt more like an interrogation than an interview. It seemed increasingly likely that they might fabricate a reason to frame me.

The newly established government believed it needed to solidify its power by an all-out assault against the opposition, especially the secular left. Despite its anti-Western hostility, it also had no tolerance for the secular left. This resulted in a crackdown on leftist groups, creating a dangerous situation for nearly all of us.

Surprisingly, the new factory managing director had reached the same conclusion. In a private meeting, he informed me of the atmosphere created by my election to the committee.

"The present climate is risky. It would be to your advantage not to stay in this factory," he whispered. "I will help you in any way possible to leave quietly."

He was the last person from whom I expected to receive an offer of a way out. His stance indicated a distance between him and the factory security, the association, and some government factions. His intervention highlighted the antagonism between people who pretended to be aligned with certain sectors of the government. The following day, he arranged for my transfer to another factory, where I worked as the factory's production planning manager for the next two years.

As the war raged, a gradual change in the country's political atmosphere became apparent. The Islamic Republic of Iran's insidious attack on the opposition, which involved the arrest of many secular activists and members of the religious opposition, was intensifying.

Many of us who shared similar perspectives were deeply committed to challenging the regime's authoritarianism through non-violent political action. Our primary objective was to persuade the Iranian populace, including the religious factions, to recognize the significance of sovereignty, civil rights, and social and economic justice. We aimed to demonstrate how crucial it is to unite in action, emphasizing that unity should not merely be about shared beliefs or ideology. Imposing one's way of life on others would divide the country and render us weak and vulnerable to interference from foreign nations. With these objectives in mind, we fervently advocated for women's liberation, labour rights, union and syndicate rights, federalism, and freedom of thought and belief. We actively voiced our opinions to encourage constructive discourse within political groups, productive forces, cultural associations, student coalitions, academic alliances, and other relevant spheres of political discussion.

There came a time when my family and I felt unsafe. Eventually, in 1984, we decided I should quit my job and move to Tehran, where I began working as a project manager for a company that conducted feasibility studies for new power plants. It was a difficult period, filled with constant uncertainty, which made it harder to focus on work.

Many activists went into hiding throughout the country. As danger loomed, I tried to be discreet in public and avoid nonessential activities.

15

Capture

Despair is suffering without meaning.
Viktor Frankl

In August 1986, I was walking along a busy street in Tehran named after Mahatma Gandhi. I felt uneasy and decided to delay meeting a friend; instead, I walked around the side streets for some minutes. Torn between facing some unknown peril and the prospect of holding up my friend, I chose to go meet him. But this decision brought me more anxiety. While looking at the people passing by, I felt this might be the last time I'd see ordinary folks in ordinary places. I had the urge to say goodbye to them without actually doing so. At that moment, ironically, I was envious of people carrying on with their everyday routines.

Returning to the busy street, I noticed a few cars circling the block. Still clinging to the hope that it was all a figment of my imagination, I turned toward a jewellery store. In its window's reflection, I began to watch behind me, keenly observing the scene. What I saw signalled something dangerous about to happen that could alter the course of my life: cars had pulled to the curbs on either side of the street, and men were getting out of them. I could feel a new tension in the air. I struggled to reassure myself that these weren't the final moments of my freedom. I fought to maintain an optimistic outlook. Each second seemed to stretch longer than usual.

Initially, the men's attempts to appear inconspicuous were effective. One of them walked close beside me, discreetly holding my wrist in such a way that I could hardly move my right hand. Others, a few steps back, pretended to be casual but eventually gave up trying to disguise their behaviour. As they intently watched my every move, we approached a car. A man in the back seat was hunched over, head resting against his thighs, face hidden. One of the men on the driver's side opened the back door.

"Get in!"

As I sat in, I looked at the man beside me. His legs were tightly wrapped below the knee, swollen to twice the normal size. It seemed as if he had been flogged, possibly with an electric cable. He lifted his head and looked at me in a way I'll never forget – a look filled with regret. For a moment, our eyes locked. I recognized him, and assumed his presence was to ensure a positive identification.

The moment I entered the car, their demeanour shifted abruptly. The facade of casual acquaintance was instantly discarded, laying bare their true, menacing intentions.

"Put your head down!" one shouted, his voice brimming with urgency and threat.

He threw a jacket over my head as the car took off. The mind works wonders. I was focused on what they might do and how I should react in return. Countless times, I have recalled that moment of capture. Strangely, in times of crisis, incidentals are pushed aside. For instance, when the jacket went over my head, a pungent body odour filled my nostrils for a split second, then vanished and never returned. My mind refocused on only one thought: how should I prepare for interrogation?

The car's sirens went on intermittently, likely activated at intersections. With each sharp turn, the vehicle careened unpredictably, the speed becoming increasingly alarming. At a point, one of them pushed something under the jacket.

"Put it on!"

It was a piece of cloth with a rubber band connecting each end, most likely used by many others before me. I had no idea this object would be part of my wardrobe for years to come. The car came to a screeching halt while I put the blindfold on. I had no illusion that my encounter with them or others like them would end quickly. It was clear that further horrifying ordeals awaited me. While expecting someone to come for me, various thoughts rushed through my mind: *What will they ask? How should I reply? Am I going to receive the same treatment as the man beside me?*

To regain my mental balance, I drew strength from my father's courage in upholding his principles and my grandmother's confidence in life. Their actions, such as my father's steadfastness in confronting the opium cartel and my grandmother's fearless lobbying of the prime minister, inspired me. I also recalled how my grandmother stood her ground despite my grandfather's condescending behaviours. These memories were a powerful guiding light, emotionally engaging me and empowering me to face the challenges ahead.

Without warning, a forceful hand yanked me from the car and propelled me toward an entrance. I was abruptly shoved into a changing room and handed a set of drab pyjamas.

"Put these on!" he said.

Then we went to a different area with much commotion. It sounded like people were being ordered around. I strained to hear and could sense people leaving the room.

When the door closed, a person shouted aggressively, "Take the blindfold off and face the camera!"

Bright lights struck my eyes. He placed a cardboard make-shift mug-shot sign on my chest with a number written on it. A camera clicked.

"Turn to the side!"

They took more pictures and eventually fingerprinted me.

"Put your blindfold back on!"

I was led out of the room. My heart was pounding, unsure of what would come next.

While being ushered into a corridor, I could see below the lower edge of my blindfold: several people, each draped in a blanket, lined either side of a long, foreboding hallway. When we came to a vacant space, my escort yelled in a jarring tone, "Lie down here!"

He placed an army blanket over my head and body while I removed my blindfold and positioned myself sideways, facing the wall. Initially, in an odd way, it created a temporary relief from the unpleasantness of the blindfold. Also, feeling briefly unattended was emotionally a respite after the intense hours since being grabbed off the street. However, after a few minutes, I felt the heaviness of the air. I clasped my hands under the blanket and made a triangle with my arms, creating a small air pocket. I wondered how long I would be under this blanket.

The first period of waiting was tolerable. It gave me time to attune myself to the day's traumatic experience. Then, time passed exceptionally slowly. The feeling of being confined in such an intense fashion was almost unbearable. Also, not knowing the number of days I might be under the blanket brought added psychological stress. The only bright side to this dreadful situation was not being claustrophobic. As time passed, I became extremely sleepy; maybe this was a survival mechanism.

It must have been around 1 a.m. or 2 a.m. when someone called my name.

"Put your blindfold on and stand up," he shouted. Then he grabbed my arm and took me to a room. As he was leaving, he said, "Sit down."

I peeked under the bottom of the blindfold and located a small wooden chair. The door closed, and I found myself alone. Every second felt like an hour. Anticipation was acting as a catalytic agent – I thought of many possible scenarios and situations. However, what amazed me was the enhanced sharpness of my mind. Finally, the door opened. A few people entered the room. Their voices came from different directions.

"Doctor, what should we do with him?" one asked.

It appeared that his question was directed to the main interrogator. Later, I discovered that the previous regime's interrogators also used inflated titles such as "Doctor" and the like. They must have believed that such bogus labels created angst for victims.

One thing I learned from that day was that determination is crucial in rescuing oneself from falling into a deep crevasse. Believing in something is imperative, regardless of the belief or cause. In our quest to discover our genuine conviction, we find our motivation. And so, resistance can become enticing and a cure for despair. We can't avoid suffering, but we can manage and find meaning in it.

I knew my whole being was about to be put to a terrible test, and I could either capitulate or resist. At that second, I felt buoyant – a sensation like being high. It's puzzling how fear and feeling determined work together. My mind was completely focused and totally in the moment. Yet I had no idea what to expect. However, before going to the interrogation room, I had decided to respond only to what I was asked and not offer anything more.

The main interrogator grabbed a chair, placed it close to me, and sat down.

"Give me names," he demanded.

I only gave him the name of the person who had identified me at the time of capture.

"You take me for a fool. I need new names."

"That's the only person I know."

He laughed and punched me hard in the chest.

"We can make life miserable for you if you don't co-operate. You might never see your family again." His words hung heavy in the air.

I was silent. Although I was sure he had some information about me from the person I had mentioned, I stayed with my strategy of giving short replies.

When he said, "You might never see your family again," I knew he wasn't bluffing; it could've happened. But overthinking it wouldn't have changed anything; it would only deflate my spirit. My family was and is the joy of my life and everything to me. The thought of how they would go through the first days of my not being alive was unbearable; they would have been devastated.

Throughout many intense interrogations, the inquisitor persistently accused me of being part of a secular opposition group, a charge I vehemently denied. This group, along with others, were rounded up across the country, allegedly due to being at odds with the regime.

During the gruelling interrogations, which often went on for fifteen to twenty minutes, the primary aim was to extract more names of like-minded individuals who peacefully opposed their authoritarian rule; my focus, however, was to resist such efforts. Sometimes, they would ask the same questions in writing, hoping to find contradictions in my responses. Yet, amid this pressure, I discovered a surprising detail about myself: my ability to think quickly had significantly improved.

Before my capture, I had heard of many people's lives destroyed by being named. A grim thought persistently haunted me. What if I survived this ordeal by a rare chance and were set free? Would I judge my behaviour in prison as acceptable? At the same time, the thought of facing the consequences of non-compliance burdened my mind. However, I knew that shouldering the psychological fallout of compliance was unquestionably more unbearable. I had seen people coerced into coming on national TV and reading their so-called statements of remorse. Their actions were understandable; not everyone resists intense pressure the same way. Nonetheless, I wondered how far into the future they would carry the personal impact of their actions.

I had many questions: Is there a limit to a person's capacity to endure pressure? What is the distinction between people who resist to the point of perishing and others who don't? During every interrogation, my ardent hope was not to be forced to test the limits of my resistance. These concerns were the sources of my constant torment. However, what gave me some comfort and hope was the thought of trying to find in myself what Albert Camus expressed: "In the middle of winter, I, at last, discovered that there was in me an invincible summer."

After a week of relentless interrogation, which involved being shuffled daily between different rooms and back under the blanket, I was finally transferred to a solitary cell. The interrogation sessions also changed to almost every other day. This cell, about 3 metres long and 2 metres wide, was devoid of windows. The immediate sensation of being liberated from the blanket was so intense that the surrounding space felt refreshing. I could look around again, enjoy standing up, and experience the pleasure of taking a few steps. The sense of relief and freedom was overwhelming. Long periods of solitary confinement are considered one of the severest forms of torture, but compared to the blanket, it was unquestionably preferable.

Since this cell didn't have a toilet, I was allowed to use the adjacent bathroom thrice daily. Walking in for the first time, I noticed a window near the ceiling with heavy horizontal and vertical steel bars inserted in front of the glass. The incoming light that filtered through the spaces between the bars was dazzlingly beautiful; it resembled rays coming through a prism. After the blanket, absorbing the piercing sun and its warmth was so restoring that if I could, I would have stood there for hours.

Following that moment of joy, I tried to find clues regarding my whereabouts. I stood on tiptoes and tried to look through the window. Surprisingly, I saw the telecommunication dishes of a famous square in Tehran. Instantly, I knew where I was: downtown.

Later, while conversing with older prisoners who had experienced this place during the previous regime, they told me it had been run by the Anti-sabotage Joint Committee (ASJC). The police, the gendarmerie, and SAVAK had formed this joint committee to counter the opposition.[1] During my stay there, some old prisoners called it *Seh-hezar* (Three Thousand in Farsi) detention centre, the meaning of which I've never found out. The general public still call it by its previous official name (now ASJC has become a museum). I also heard from the same older prisoners that the building was designed in an *X* shape. Apparently, during the Shah's time, most of the interrogations occurred in the middle of the *X*. And so, when someone was to be tortured, they would say, "He went *zire-hasht*," which means below or under eight (the bottom half of the *X* looks the same as the number eight in Farsi).

By the third week, the frequency of my interrogations changed to once or twice a week. As a result, they moved me from solitary to a room with about twenty other people. At first, living in one room with many prisoners required some adjustment. Few inmates encouraged discussion about our recent arrest and its aftermath. At that time, I wasn't familiar with the complexities of the prison environment and the risk of trusting others. Therefore, I went with my gut feeling and remained reserved, especially when the extent of other prisoners' co-operation with the authorities was unclear. Later, though, I realized that mistrusting others, while understandably necessary in the circumstances, had enormous costs – I sacrificed valuable and rare relationships with some who were the best of the best.

While enduring the harsh conditions of solitary confinement, I found a brief respite in the illusion of time passing faster. However, this changed as soon as I became accustomed to communal life. It's ironic: all through life, the fantasy of wanting time to slow down is enticing. Yet, in trying times, the opposite is true. Being among a seemingly compatible group and seeing others in the same predicament gave me a semblance of a shared burden and lessened the stress.

Moreover, the relief of relocating to a more spacious area and improving my living conditions provided much-needed comfort. Now, I had three blankets. I could lie on one; the second was my pillow, and the third covered me.

A few days passed. I recall one difficult night. We were about to fall asleep when we heard a girl sobbing from a nearby room – men and women were kept in separate rooms, but unlike a formal prison, this facility didn't use different wards for segregation. It appeared that she was being bombarded with questions. The conversation between her and someone else was inaudible, but her cries were unmistakably clear. As soon as an answer was deemed unsatisfactory, she received a firm slap. We couldn't tell how she was struck, but it was most likely with a slipper. It continued for some time, and her anguish was unbearable. As I looked around, I saw no one had slept. It was early in the morning when her cries finally stopped. Was this episode deliberately designed to create a fearful atmosphere, or were the authorities indifferent to us knowing about it?

That whole night, listening to her, I thought of the pain she endured. Throughout history, people like her are easily labelled undesirable, making them worthy of suffering or elimination. I wondered what would become of the girl. Would she come out of this ordeal alive? If so, could she cope with the trauma, marry, have children, and live a peaceful life? I thought of the interrogators' inability to place a face on people different from them due to their entrenched biases, or maybe some are motivated by opportunistic ambitions.

Another week passed. One of the occupants of our room had gone for interrogation. He returned with a piece of paper on which a list of names was jotted down. He showed us the poorly handwritten list.

"They want these five people and me to get ready for a conversation with a former well-known secular activist."

My name was on the list. It seemed they aimed to use him to lure us into co-operation. They likely assumed that offering a way out could be enticing in dire situations, especially if a so-called like-minded individual suggested it. Due to our harsh conditions, they also counted on the element of fatigue as an agent of persuasion.

After a brief conversation, we all decided that engaging with this person would be fruitless. It would only give the authorities more information about us. Therefore, we agreed to accept the risks and boycott him by not participating in his discussions.

Two hours later, they called out our names.

"Put your blindfolds on and walk in one line."

We were led to a larger room and told to sit on a rug close to a corner. A man in his thirties had already established himself on the edge of the rug with his back to the wall: medium-statured, dark-haired, clean-shaven with a large moustache. His eyes scanned the room and then watched as we found our places, sitting in a circle. He began his rant.

"I want you to know that my decision not to play the hero game didn't come easy. I've thought about it hard and long," he said. "It's useless; they know a lot about us. Don't be fools by putting yourselves in danger. Think about your families, especially your children. The authorities have assured me that all of you can go home tomorrow if you come to your senses."

After more of his rant, he asked if we had any questions. Given our previous decision to boycott him, I anticipated a period of silence. To my extreme surprise, four individuals, one after the other, began to ask questions. This unexpected turn of events was an epiphany that profoundly influenced my future conduct in prison. Why did they change their minds? Did they want to mitigate their situation? Was it a tactic or due to fear? Were they so naive as to believe even part of his argument? Is it possible that in harsh conditions where one is constantly tested, we have no alternative but to show our true selves eventually? How should I react to them after this?

Once the meeting was over, we returned to our room. I decided to ignore their actions. I had become extremely cautious and knew that discussing the subject would only result in disclosing something of myself to individuals who couldn't be trusted.

The religious opposition were kept separate, leaving only secular individuals in our room. We quickly learned to avoid discussing what went on during our interrogation sessions. As recent detainees, we weren't inclined to socialize extensively anyway, and besides, we had to be wary of potential collaborators. Instead, we focused on maintaining a semblance of normalcy, engaging in light conversations and mental games like solving puzzles and even reciting poetry to each other. Our days were spent mainly preparing for the next interrogation.

At this point, our families were completely unaware of our whereabouts.

I remember asking a man seated close to me, whom I had known for a few days, how he was holding up.

"Not too well," he said dispiritedly. "There are so many unknowns that I have no idea what will happen to me. My future is totally up to them."

As he shared his worries, I found myself nodding in agreement. I tried to console him, though it was a feeling we both knew too well.

Mornings were a brief respite. New faces would arrive, and others would leave, providing a temporary distraction from overthinking. But most evenings were a different story. The fear of not knowing the limits of my resilience and the dread of potentially reaching it during interrogation were the most haunting thoughts that swirled in my mind.

Each day, around 7 a.m., we would receive our breakfast: feta cheese, bread, and tea. Lunch was usually rice with some casserole; dinner was soup or rice again. These mealtimes, though predictable, did little to lift our spirits. Given the poor quality of the food and the weight of our circumstances, many of us had little interest in eating.

It had been around ten or eleven days since my last interrogation, and the setting for this particular encounter was markedly different from what I had experienced before. I remember that moment vividly to this day. I was summoned to meet my main interrogator. As I stepped into the room, below the bottom of my blindfold, I noticed a small rug that covered around seventy percent of the floor, with the rest bare cement tiles. He was seated on the rug, reclining casually on a backrest, sipping tea; his demeanour was surprisingly laid-back given the circumstances. I could only see his feet; his shoes, similar to penny loafers, were placed near the edge of the rug. I was uncertain if others were in the room.

"Don't let him sit on the rug," the interrogator told the guard. "A heathen is unclean and not purified. If you aren't careful, his body might touch the rug. Then, I'd have to send it out to be washed."

I wondered if he genuinely believed his words or if it was just a ploy to humiliate me. Although this gesture, in comparison to many others, was one of his milder courses of action, all the same, maybe by piling up different techniques, he was trying to prod me to react eventually. Regardless, being silent was the best way to neutralize his aggression. I sat on the bare cement tiles about 30 centimetres from the rug.

I answered the usual questions during the interrogation with short sentences and no additional comments. He appeared annoyed, and after about ten minutes, he called the guard to take me back to my room. At first, I thought that his attitude of belittling me didn't affect me. However, the fact that this episode still stands out in my mind affirms that he made his mark.

About a month later, around mid-morning, I was again called for interrogation. When the main interrogator came in, I recognized him by his shoes – the style and their red cherry-wood colour. This seemingly insignificant detail had a profound effect on my psyche. A Pavlovian association surfaced. Later, when I came across the same type of shoes in Evin Prison, it would trigger a vivid and distressing flashback.

"We have your brother!" His words were like a thunderclap, shattering the tense silence that had been building in the room.

Instantly, I lost my composure and pulled up my blindfold. For a few seconds, I saw his face. Then, out of nowhere, someone aggressively came toward me.

"Put it back on!"

Unexpectedly, the main interrogator switched roles, becoming the "good cop" and ordering the other man, "Leave him alone!" Then, just as abruptly, he said, "Put the blindfold on!"

After putting the blindfold back on, I regained my composure and could think coherently. I told him I would believe it if I saw my brother in person. I received no reaction. It's interesting how, in extreme situations, we examine every detail in our minds. In less than a few seconds, I thought of many possibilities. Were they bluffing? If not, how was my eldest brother captured? Did one of his friends turn him in? Many months later, I learned from my family, with whom I hadn't communicated for a long time, that the Doctor was right; my brother had been captured. The emotional journey of not knowing and the lack of communication with my family was a heavy burden to bear.

"Why didn't you tell us about him?" asked the Doctor.

"We only discussed politics in general. Our day-to-day life was not part of our usual conversation," I replied, my voice steady and unwavering.

I didn't see my brother until some time later in Evin Prison.

16
Evin

Freedom is what you do with what's been done to you.
Jean-Paul Sartre

I was interrogated intermittently for about two and a half months. The uncertainty of what they would eventually do with me was a constant source of tension. Any change was better than the present situation; even the mere absence of interrogation for the past two weeks was a huge relief. People were coming and going from the room every day, but for a few of us, nothing changed.

Then, one day, four names were called, including mine.

"Put your blindfolds on and come out," the jailer said.

We were told to change our clothes, dressing in what we had on when we were captured, and then led to a van. After three long months, it seemed like we were finally leaving the infamous Three Thousand. I had yet to learn where we were going, but in a strange way, I was pleased about the change. Maybe it was the prospect of not seeing my interrogators, especially the Doctor. As we drove toward our new destination, I thought of the unfathomable hardship I had endured during the past three months. The emotional toll of the experience was immense, but the most crucial factor, which gave me some consolation, was that I had no part in furnishing the jailers with new information.

After about twenty minutes, we reached the notorious Evin Prison. I was led through a labyrinth of stairs and hallways and finally into a solitary cell. What immediately grabbed my attention was the way this edifice was built. Later, older prisoners told me that the knowledge gained regarding psychological confinement techniques during the Vietnam War and elsewhere was incorporated into the design of Evin when constructed in 1971.

As I removed my blindfold, the metal door behind me shut. The door had a peephole at eye level and another opening at the bottom for dispensing food. I saw rays of natural light coming through a 60-square-centimetre opening in the ceiling, about 3.5 metres above me. However, it was set at an angle, so one couldn't see the sky. The cell was a little less than 3 metres long by 2 metres wide. In one corner, close to the metal door, there stood a small sink with a faucet attached to the wall above it. On the same long side, next to the sink, was an inverted conical bowl that served as the latrine. Behind it was a U-shaped pipe, about 10 centimetres in diameter and 1 metre long, a heating conduit connected to all the cells. It wasn't long before I noticed something noteworthy: the heating pipes were an efficient way for prisoners who knew Morse code to transmit information. Opposite the pipe on the other side of the cell was an area on the floor that could accommodate a blanket folded on its longer side.

Three times a day, the jailers would open my cell door's bottom flap and yell, "Turn around and face the wall."

This technique was meant to deprive us of our basic need to see another human being. The tray of food was placed on the floor; often the bread was tossed near the latrine in a blatant attempt to humiliate us and show their dominance. However, they failed to realize that humiliating determined individuals generally strengthens rather than weakens their resolve.

Right from the outset, I rigorously scheduled every moment to bolster my mood. My routine occupied most of my waking hours and was a critical technique for coping with the brutality of isolation. However, when special occasions arose, I would eagerly stray from the usual timetable; for instance, when I watched an ant move across the floor and manoeuvre around obstacles, the spectacle was tantamount to meditation. Or when, in the springtime, the migrating parrots flew over my cell, their beautiful calls to each other instantly mesmerized me and reminded me of my childhood walks in nature.

Usually, though, first thing in the morning, I would wash my face and upper body. Then, I would have my meagre breakfast of feta cheese, a piece of bread, and a cup of tea. The bottom flap would open for the jailer to take the dishes back. Afterward, I was ready for exercise, which involved push-ups, squats, toe touches, jumping jacks, and more. It would last at least half an hour, and I would repeat it in the afternoon. Then, I would start designing an imaginary integrated total system for a manufacturing company, including material handling, inventory, production, and quality control entities. All subsystems would operate in coordination with the total system as a network. This routine, while monotonous, provided a sense of structure and purpose to my days. I timed my finish so that I would rest for a few minutes before lunchtime.

Next, someone would yell, "Face the wall!" This meant that the top hatch of the steel door would open to ensure I was facing away. Then, the jailer would open the bottom hatch and place my lunch on the floor. It usually consisted of a piece of bread, a casserole on top of rice or a bowl of soup, and a cup of tea. After lunch, for at least an hour, I would try to remember my earlier life in detail.

During my darkest days, I found refuge in the transformative power of music and poetry. One well-known song, "Mara Beboos" (Kiss Me), composed during the Shah's regime in the 1950s, helped me immensely. It depicts the last days of a political prisoner bidding farewell to his daughter. It starts with, "Kiss me for the last time." Somehow, singing this song allowed me to empathize deeply with the protagonist's plight, calming me profoundly. The emotional connection I felt with the song was so intense that it made me feel like I was living the story myself. Similarly, I also recited in Farsi a fourteenth-century poem by Hafiz; its heartfelt wisdom helped me gain more mental toughness in the face of adversity. This is my translation in English:

> If the keeper of the garden is to entertain the blooming flowers and yet still not be deterred by his brief engagement.
> He must have the patience of a Nightingale to withstand the anguish brought by the thorn of his estrangement.
> Oh, my tender heart, don't despair and weep for a lock of her hair.
> Once the cunning bird befalls capture, forbearance is the remedy to bear.

At times, I would think about Pegah and our relationship. In the early days of our marriage, after her work, she would eagerly revisit the events of her day with me. I thought about our conversations and wondered if, by chance, I got out of this wretched place, would I continue to enjoy talking with her like before, up into our old age? I wondered about the magic of conversation – would it endure the twists and turns of our lives? Would we, in due course, grow even closer, or would we grow apart?

After a while, I lost count of how long I'd been in isolation. I could see lines on the wall that suggested others before me had counted their time. One group of marks revealed 153 days. Was the recorder released after etching the last one, or was it the final line before entering darkness? Although I had been in the cell for a shorter period, I played a mind game and gave myself the same number of days. It would be a mental triumph if my actual time were shorter than I had imagined.

Having no contact with anyone for so long, it did become clear that once I had left Three Thousand, I had completed my interrogation period, which was a huge relief.

I found an inscription on the wall: "When words remain in your mind, they're your slave; when uttered out, you are their slave."

The anonymous author was trying to express the reality that those who experience interrogation face. Did this individual spend a long time here? Which regime captured her or him? Is this person alive or gone, like many others? In an instant, my thoughts pictured us in one room. *Oh, if only we could have shared our many untold stories.*

I was interrupted by a loud voice.

"Turn around and face the wall."

It seemed strange to me, as it was too early for dinner. After closing the peephole, the jailer opened the door.

"Put your blindfold on and come out with all your belongings."

The feeling of emerging from isolation is hard to express. It's like travelling from a remote place to a hectic city. The commotion of the present moment temporarily suspends the unpleasant memory of the immediate past.

I walked behind him for some time as we went downstairs into an open area. Eventually, we entered a four-storey building and stopped in front of a room on the ground floor. He unlocked the door.

"Get in!"

Later, I was told by the older prisoners that this building was used as offices for the prison staff during the previous regime. It was adjacent to the solitary confinement building, called *Asayeshgah* (Tranquility Ward). The former was on the east side, and the latter on the north. Both buildings overlooked a large swimming pool, most likely used by the previous regime's staff. These buildings were atop a hill, looking down on the rest of Evin. During the Shah's regime, all prison wards were located at the bottom of the hill, now called Band-a Ghadeem (Old Wards).

As I entered, I took my blindfold off. To my surprise, I saw about thirty other prisoners in a room approximately 8 metres long and 4 metres wide. A bunk bed in the front left corner of the room had many rolled-up blankets on the top bunk. A big window opposite the door had angled horizontal metal sheets welded at each end to the window frame. The gaps between the sheets were wide enough to partially see a yard. On the right side of the room, alongside the wall, were other rolled-up blankets. Aside from some prisoners standing around and others slowly walking from one side to the other, few were seated on their blankets.

The first few hours in the room starkly contrasted the solitude I had grown accustomed to. The transition from isolation to a crowded space was challenging, and I grappled with the sudden change. However, I was determined to adapt by speeding up this process and, most importantly, distract myself from overwhelming thoughts. During this time, someone approached me, introduced himself, and asked my name.

"You can put your belongings here," he said. "It can also be your sleeping area."

What I had with me were just three blankets, the clothes I wore during capture, and a pair of slippers I had brought with me from Three Thousand. My shoes and the contents of my pockets were still with the prison administration.

As I considered my next step, a short, stocky man approached and whispered, "My name is Bijan. Have you been captured long?" Upon hearing my response, his face softened with empathy and murmured, "We're all in this together. You're not alone."

As time passed, I had many exchanges with various people. Some were just being sociable; others asked peculiar questions, like "Are you going to sign a statement of remorse?" which at first appeared innocuous. My answer was always an emphatic no. Initially, I wasn't aware that there might have been an ulterior motive behind such a question. At that time, I had no idea why we were all gathered in one place. However, shortly after my transfer, I became suspicious and convinced that our time spent in that room, which seemed like a revolving door, was, in all likelihood, part of a final assessment process, a way to decide how to distribute us to the "appropriate" ward. And so, in our midst, they must have had a few embedded *Tavabs* (collaborators/repentants).

The authority's strategy was to put more like-minded people in the same ward so that the less compliant prisoners wouldn't influence the others. Later, I discovered that there were also different degrees of Tavabs, from those who conspired with the authorities to those who had just given up.

As I continued my stay on the first floor of the north wing, I encountered numerous difficulties, particularly during the initial nights. The sleeping area, often a mere half-metre wide due to the number of occupants, forced individuals like me, with broad shoulders, to adapt and sleep on our side. The need to fall asleep quickly to avoid a symphony of snores was a constant struggle. Yet, the anticipation of what lay ahead throughout my imprisonment always loomed large and trumped many physical hardships.

The rules of this room were less stringent. We were taken to a washroom three times a day and allowed a walk in the yard once daily, usually around 11 a.m., for about twenty minutes. My first experience stepping into a yard was a breath of fresh air. After many months of being indoors, I could feel the open space, an irresistible sensation. I took a whiff of fresh air and was transported to another world – a feeling of sharper sensory receptiveness. Looking around, I saw bricks and concrete covering the entire yard. The walls soared up more than 6 metres, and the only sign of nature to enjoy was the blue sky and the clouds. Despite these limitations, there were moments when I escaped from my usual thoughts, ascended toward the clouds, and drifted out of that wretched place. Oh, how I yearned never to come back. At that moment, having no worries, a feeling of calm engulfed my whole body, which I hadn't felt for some time.

As winter approached, the weather grew colder. I had had no family visitations, so received no extra clothing from my immediate family – items were only sent if approved by the authorities. Eventually, I could correspond with my family, but the process of writing and sending letters was quite strict.

We were given a form 20 centimetres long by 14 centimetres wide, and there were limitations on the number of lines we could use – only seven lines to write on. After finishing our letter, it was sent to the prison authorities for censoring and mailing. If the authorities found anything objectionable, the letter would be returned with a note on top of the letter explaining why. If deemed acceptable and sent on, our family would write on the back of the same form. If the censors found something inappropriate in our family's messages, they would warn the prisoner or would keep it. I was only able to write and receive about twenty-two letters over nearly three years. Letter writing was done monthly during the more lenient periods, but there were times when it was suspended for months. Despite the challenges, the value of these letters cannot be overstated.

In my initial letter, I informed my family about how to respond. I focused on assuring them of my well-being, although I wasn't sure if they believed me. I mentioned the possibility of visitations and how I eagerly anticipated seeing them after many months. The first letter Pegah and my parents received from me was a joint letter; afterwards, they received separate letters.

Their first reply was exhilarating.

"There is not a day that our son and I don't think of the good times we had with you," Pegah wrote. "We always talk about the day of your freedom and how dearly we love and miss you. I promise to raise our son as best as possible."

My parents' response was also filled with affection and reassurance: "Our only wish in life is your freedom, and we want to assure you that with all our love for you, we will take care of your son; he is the light of our life."

After that, whenever my name was called to receive a letter, it felt like a bad dream was ending or I had found my way out of a frustrating maze.

In another letter, Pegah adapted a verse from a poem and wrote: "A swallow – your son – has sheltered on the eave of

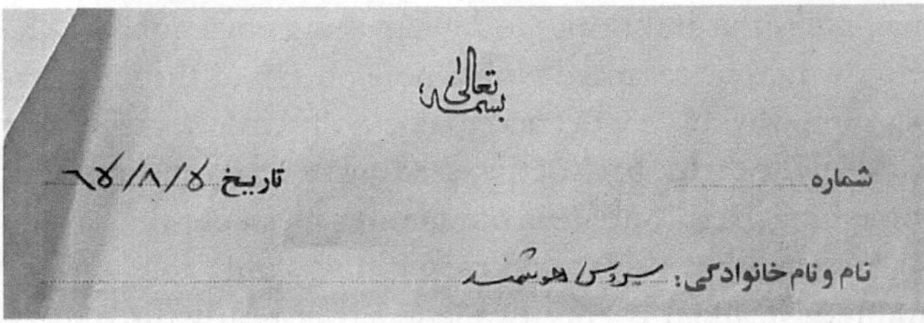

بسمه تعالی

شماره .... تاریخ ۶۵/۸/۵

نام و نام خانوادگی: سیروس هوشمند

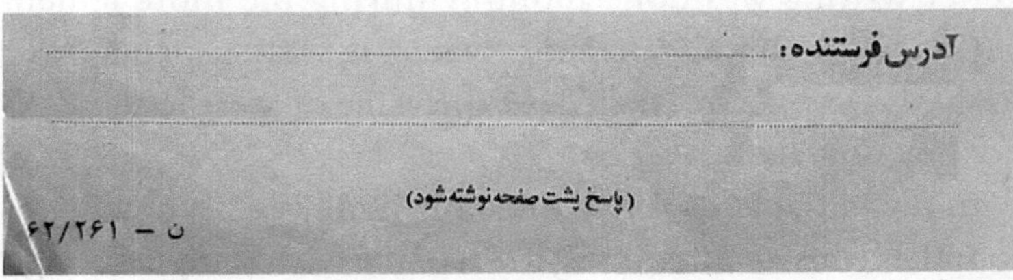

آدرس فرستنده:

(پاسخ پشت صفحه نوشته شود)

ن – ۶۲/۲۶۱

بسمه تعالی

شماره .... تاریخ ....

نسبت پاسخ دهنده نامه با زندانی:

آدرس و مشخصات پاسخ دهنده:

Figure 16.1 *Opposite, top to bottom*
The front and back sides of an official prison form that needed to be completed to write and receive letters while incarcerated at Evin.

Front of form, top. First line: The right side has the word "Number" typed in Farsi. The left side has the word "Date" typed in Farsi (in Farsi, I wrote in: 27 October 1986). Second line: The typed Farsi words request "First and last name" (in Farsi, I wrote in: Sirous Houshmand). Below the second line were seven numbered lines for the prisoner's message.

Front of form, bottom. The first line, right side, has the words "Address of sender" typed in Farsi, followed by a blank line to the left and one below for the building name, ward, and room number of the prisoner. In the middle of the third line is a directive in parentheses typed in Farsi: "Reply must be written on the back of this form." The last line on the left is an internal form number.

Back of form, top. First line: Again, typed in Farsi, the right side has the word "Number" and the left side the word "Date," with blank space to fill in that information. Second line: The typed Farsi words request "The relationship of the individual replying to the prisoner," with a blank line for that information. Below that were seven numbered lines for a reply.

Back of form, bottom. The first line, right side, has the words "Address and specification of respondent" typed in Farsi, followed by blank lines for that information.

your roof and calls for you repeatedly." I read the passage over and over; my heart ached for a moment of caressing his innocent face, knowing that his suffering was through no fault of his own.

The combination of my imprisonment and the pain it caused my family was a constant torment for me. I couldn't stop thinking about my four-year-old son and how much he needed me. At the same time, I grappled with and rejected the idea of choosing between my love for him, my family, and my commitment to my values. It wasn't about selecting one or the other – why couldn't both simultaneously be central to my life? Yet the inner conflict it caused was deeply complex, with layers of emotions that I struggled to navigate.

The number of people in our room fluctuated. Every few days, new prisoners would arrive, and others would be taken away. I'd been there over a month when a man called out my name.

"Put your blindfold on and come out with all your belongings!"

I followed him to a wide foyer, the sound of our footsteps reverberating in the empty space, and climbed the stairs to the fourth floor. The off-odour of the building filled my nostrils. He unlocked a door and said, "Take your blindfold off."

We entered a very crowded hallway with many people roaming around. He took me to the south end, turned right, and said, "This is your room."

Several people came forward and introduced themselves. One, whose expression radiated kindness, said, "My name is Naser. Sit here and relax. You must have endured a lot by now."

With a heart full of gratitude, I enquired about my new location.

"You are in *Sallon-a Shesh* (Ward Six)," he answered.

The layout of my new room, along with the number of occupants, seemed similar to the previous one, except there was no bunk bed. After spending some time there, I decided to explore the rest of the ward. For the first time in months, I could walk around freely, without a blindfold, in a spacious area for as long as I pleased. The sense of freedom was invigorating.

I entered the long hallway and proceeded north. I noticed at least five rooms on each side with people moving to and fro. At the end of this hallway was a medium-sized washroom on the west side and a smaller room on the east side. What immediately grabbed my attention was the cleanliness of the ward.

Every week, a democratic process was followed to select five people from one room to clean the common areas. A week later, the next room had its turn. This system ensured the ward's cleanliness and fostered a sense of responsibility and community. Every day, the volunteers washed the hallway and the bathroom. The saying about the hallway's spotlessness was, "If you drop something on the floor, you'll be okay if you eat it."

Despite the challenging circumstances, most prisoners displayed remarkable adaptability in their daily tasks. The volunteers, who served food and handled everyday chores in each room, also rotated weekly. This system, known as *mellie-karie* (national work), was a legacy of the political prisoners of the Shah's regime, and its name was maintained to show respect and honour their memory.

Our ward was in the south wing of the four-storey building, and men occupied most wings except one. Over time, I gathered enough information to make a few assumptions about the prison authorities' reasoning for separating prisoners into different wards. It seemed that prisoners were assigned to a particular ward based on their perceived level of compliance. However, there may have been some cases where the authorities' evaluations were incorrect.

The first floor of the south wing, *Sallon-a Yek* (Ward One), was where Tavabs resided. They wore prison clothes and were tasked with making clothing, cabinets, and other products in workshops as well as performing kitchen duties, gardening, and other chores that the prison authorities dictated. On the second floor of the same wing was *Sallon-a Doh* (Ward Two), where inmates also worked in workshops while wearing prison clothes. Above Ward Two was *Sallon-a Chahar* (Ward Four), where individuals wore street clothes and could work in the same workshops or independently carry out approved industrial or scientific projects. Finally, above Ward Four was *Sallon-a Shesh* (Ward Six), where individuals did not wear prison clothes or work in any capacity the authorities imposed or approved.

It later became clear to me that the authorities' temporary leniency and change of tactics toward Ward Six were partly due to some of the previous inmates' resistance by refusing to submit despite the former warden's brutal approach. In retrospect, their suffering brought periods of respite for many of us. The authorities' failure to achieve their goals likely led to their new strategy of instability, fluctuating between extreme and moderate pressure, keeping us in a constant state of uncertainty.

The design of the north wing of our building was like the south wing. The first floor, where I was, was used as a first stage to test or assess the prisoners. The second floor of the same wing was *Sallon-a Seh* (Ward Three). At that time, this floor was vacant. Other prisoners had informed me that the previous warden had transferred all its occupants to Gohardasht, the prison 40 kilometres from Tehran. Their relocation came after a display of defiance, a remarkable act of bravery. Reportedly, both prisons were brutal; however, I was unsure of the outcome of this transfer.

Above Ward Three was *Sallon-a Panj* (Ward Five), the women's ward. They were entirely separate from us to the extent that we might only catch a glimpse of them accidentally in the hallways of the infirmary. My knowledge of how they were treated or managed was scant, but it most likely couldn't have differed vastly from our experiences. The only thing that caught my eye was that they were forced to wear a black veil. The other floor of the north wing remained a mystery to me.

While getting acquainted with my new environment, I noticed a network of classes in progress. The occupants of the ward organized them without any involvement of the authorities. Different groups convened daily to study and learn English, literature, poetry, grammar, handwriting, calligraphy, history, handicrafts, and other subjects. It wasn't long before I joined in as an English teacher, overseeing the highest level, which dealt with conversational skills. I had two people face each other and discuss an assigned topic. Every day, these types of sessions would continue for hours. I was a student of Farsi grammar, handwriting, and calligraphy.

The level of organization of the classes and the attention given to maintaining the ward were impressive. The jailers' pressure tactics, while challenging, motivated us. It was a passive-aggressive way of resisting authorities and demonstrating that political prisoners can lead a different way of life. It seemed that most of the inmates in Ward Six were determined to show that there was a cultural difference between us and them.

I soon learned that in Ward Six, people were, as a rule, allowed visitations once every two weeks, with some exceptions. However, only a small percentage of us were ever called since many factors had a bearing, such as prisoners or their families being punished, prisoners without visitors, or families living outside of Tehran who couldn't easily travel. So, it was a delightful surprise whenever my name was called for a visit. Throughout my time in Ward Six, this privilege was only allowed during calmer periods and was suspended at other times, making each visitation a moment of pure happiness.

The first sight of Pegah and my mother on the other side of a window was a powerful experience, filling me with a mix of emotions: disbelief, joy, and a tinge of sadness.

"How is your health?" my mother asked, her voice filled with concern, after she picked up the phone. Her question, though simple, carried a world of love and worry.

Before I could respond, my wife inquired, "Are you eating well?"

"Don't worry about me!" I said. "I'm fine, but I need warmer clothes."

A few tears moved down their cheeks.

"You've lost weight," my wife whispered concernedly.

"Yes, but I'm gaining it back. How is my father?"

"Seeing you on the other side of the window is too much for his age," my mother said while crying. "He'd be devastated. I don't think he can withstand the pain."

While holding back my emotions, I said, "You can bring warm clothes on our next visit."

They nodded sorrowfully.

Throughout our conversation, an incredible sensation of bliss merged with an unbearable feeling of concern. My body trembled as I witnessed their love and suffering. Since we knew someone was listening, enjoying their presence was more urgent than an extensive conversation. After a few minutes of going over their daily life, we heard: "Visitation time is up!"

Parting was painful. As they left, I felt the absence of their voices, gestures, and beautiful eyes. The physical distance between us seemed insurmountable. I yearned to be free like the swallows, to fly off to meet them outside this dismal place!

Prisoners' children could see their parents after the visitation, but not always. This visit was one of those. My five-year-old son ran toward me, a bundle of love and energy. I held him close to my heart, feeling his love and warmth, and couldn't let go. Our bond, despite the circumstances, was unbreakable.

"Baba," he said with a sparkle in his eyes, "I've got something for you." His excitement was contagious, and I couldn't help but smile.

"What do you have?"

"I have a chocolate bar!" he softly said so others couldn't hear.

"Didn't they take it from you when you were searched?"

"No, I wore my warm-ups in reverse, so the pockets were at the back. When they searched me, I leaned against the wall. They didn't find the chocolate bar."

I've never forgotten his cheerful face when he gave it to me. He must have planned this for many days. Many in our room, except the known Tavabs, had a small piece of chocolate that day.

On another occasion, the jailers, in a more relaxed time, granted my mother her first in-person visitation (visiting without any barriers).

"Mother, why are you wearing a black *chador* [a veil covering the hair and body]?" I asked.

"I did it so maybe they treat you better!" she said, her sacrifice noticeable in her heartfelt words.

I couldn't tell her about the complexities of prison life and how it might have the opposite effect. One must walk a tightrope; her action might show weakness to jailers and a sign that pressure works. On the other hand, acting too boldly can give them an excuse to punish unnecessarily. Therefore, finding the right balance is critical. Also, I knew she wasn't comfortable with the chador and had never worn it, a struggle I couldn't share with her.

"Mother, please don't wear the chador next time," I said assertively.

"Why?"

"It won't change anything."

17
Friendship

You can hold yourself back from the sufferings of the world, that is something you are free to do and it accords with your nature, but perhaps this very holding back is the one suffering you could avoid.
Franz Kafka

A week after I arrived in Ward Six, a disturbing incident occurred. On the 19th of *Bahman* (8 February), a few inmates organized a remembrance gathering. On that day, during the Shah's regime, a political group had lost some of its members in the jungles of northern Iran. A prisoner sang a famous song called "Ghoghayeh Setaregan" (The Uproar of the Stars). The song starts: "Tonight, passion is surging from my innermost being …"

The prison guards burst into our room without warning, acting on a tip from informants, and abruptly ended the gathering. We were blindfolded and led downstairs to the building's foyer, where we were forced to stand facing the wall for the entire night. Anyone who attempted to relax their posture earned a kick and a stern command, "Don't slouch!"

As the morning light filtered in, we were called for individual interrogation. A guard spoke to me around 9 a.m.

"Turn around and come with me," he said.

As I entered a room with my blindfold on, someone yelled, “Sit down!” Then, he asked, “I want you to be frank with me. Who organized this gathering?”

“I have no idea,” I replied.

It was true. I didn’t know the answer. He repeated the same question, and I responded, “I don’t know.”

“We will eventually get it out of you,” he shouted.

Next, he told the guard to take me back to where I had stood before. It wasn’t until late afternoon that we were all escorted back into our room. I never found out if anyone was accused.

It is easy to get entangled in the ignorance of what is happening behind closed doors and other prisoners’ planning. I can understand the desire to pursue a cause, especially when one feels connected to its decision-making. However, I quickly learned that without independent thinking, one can get into trouble and not know why. The difficulty of distinguishing between genuine inmates and informants is a constant threat; a few who, on the surface, gave the impression of being defiant and courageous in situations like this weren’t exactly what they appeared to be. There were occasions where their bravado was too ostentatious to be credible.

Suspicion contaminates relationships, robbing one of the joys of associating with some of the finest people. It was a constant battle to trust and to doubt, and I had no choice but to depend on my judgment. The emotional toll of this continuous suspicion is immense.

Another month passed when a question puzzling me was answered. What do they do with people who develop mental illness? One morning, they brought in a prisoner who couldn’t control his body discharge. Usually, these individuals buckled in solitary confinement or couldn’t handle some other kind of pressure. It became clear that we were to care for them instead of their being transferred to an institution for nursing or rehabilitation. When the guards escorted such a man into our room, we would take turns each day tending to his needs, feeding, cleaning, and restraining him from hurting himself.

After a few months, I became more accustomed to my living conditions and made significant friends. Khosrow was in his early thirties, relatively tall, broad-shouldered, and strong-looking. His receding hairline gave him a dignified and distinguished look. We were assigned to different rooms; however, a few months after my arrival in Ward Six, we ran into each other in the hallway and immediately hit it off. From then on, our friendship grew, and we found a wealth of common ground on many issues, strengthening our bond. Our shared experiences created a strong sense of camaraderie. At the same time, we knew there were limits to our conversations. Unfortunately, we had to assume it wasn't safe to fully trust anyone, which prevented us from getting too close, so we limited our discussions to philosophy and socio-economics.

A strategic and balanced approach marked Khosrow's time in prison. He upheld his principles yet was careful not to give the guards a reason to mistreat him unnecessarily. His low-key personality was a shield, but he stood firm on essential matters. His vast proficiency in Farsi, particularly evident during his classical literature sessions, was a testament to his intellect. He was cerebral yet deeply emotional when discussing the plight of the impoverished and the injustices they endured, resonating with a profound sense of humanity and empathy.

Throughout my time in Ward Six, the constant room changes were a source of intense stress, a tactic designed to disrupt our daily routines. Yet, we found ways to adapt. Sometimes, we were moved to different rooms with open doors. Other times, all doors would suddenly close, leaving no access to the hallway and other rooms, except for guided visits to the washroom twice daily. One time when the authorities decided to change our rooms, I was fortunate to be assigned to the same room as Khosrow. This period lasted for at least nine months and was the least stressful period of my prison experience.

Our mealtime was a unique experience. We would sit on the floor, half on either side of a long rectangular plastic sheet. Two individuals facing each other would share a bowl of food. Known Tavabs were excluded. Khosrow and I often faced each other, discussing the day's events. Occasionally, we would intentionally sit with others to ensure no one felt left out. Conversing with Khosrow was always a pleasure; his calm demeanour was infectious.

I remember walking together in one of the prison yards – occasionally, the entire ward was permitted to enjoy the fresh air. In those instances, political prisoners would customarily stroll the yard length in twos. Khosrow and I covered many subjects, but one that stood out was our conversation about feminism in general and specifically the struggles of women in West Asia.

"What frustrates you most about women's plight in our region?" I asked.

"The inability of women to understand the injustices afforded to them," he replied, adding, "Many even support the patriarchal norms that oppress them."

"This behaviour is embedded in various structures of power that create divisive boundaries and social maladies, which in this case is manifested as cultural failings," I said while anxiously awaiting his reply.

"Yes! And so, with the support of social privileges, some male counterparts feel free to act misogynistic." He nodded, tightening his lips, lowering his eyebrows and pulling them closer together. "If only enough men and women became aware of social injustices, including this one, then there is hope for women's emancipation," he asserted, veins protruding from his forehead and temples.

After our conversation, I was struck by the depth of Khosrow's knowledge and how far ahead of his time his thoughts were compared to many Iranian intellectuals.

On another occasion, we delved into the life and works of Omar Khayyam, the great Persian mathematician, astronomer, philosopher, and poet from the eleventh and twelfth centuries. His poetry's profound philosophical depth and lyrical beauty have left an indelible mark on Persian literature. Khosrow's mastery of Persian history, especially Khayyam, was truly remarkable.

"What do you think of his poetry?" I asked.

"As you know, many of his poems emphasize the importance of enjoying the present while it's at hand and not being overly distracted or distressed with the past or the future. Unfortunately, some people mistakenly believe that his focus on enjoying the present is a justification for inactivity. His life was dedicated to scientific achievements, discovery, and innovation. He even designed a solar calendar, which is still used as the basis for the Persian calendar," said Khosrow.

"What do you think of his courage?" I asked.

"He wrote about highly controversial subjects, which could have been grounds for prosecution and mistreatment for his time – or even now in Iran. His name was greatly respected in our house. He was one of the first whose courage affected me and made a permanent mark on my memory," said Khosrow.

My friendship with Khosrow continued for less than two years. We became very close and had many enlightening discussions until they took him away into darkness.

Another remarkable friend was Naser. He was in his late twenties, medium height, stoutly built, with straight, thick hair. Our initial encounter was when I arrived in Ward Six: he was the first person in the room to greet and comfort me. Over time, our friendship grew. Naser was remarkably frank, his honesty evident in every interaction. His level of truthfulness was a rarity, a quality I had never come across before. Throughout my life, I've met a few people who, through manipulation, furthered their so-called friendship. Naser was the opposite; his nature was devoid of any craftiness, his incorruptibility and purity of heart shining through. Our close relationship was less intellectual and more visceral. When faced with pressure from the guards, we would comfort each other, turning our friendship into a refuge that strengthened our resolve.

Naser's personality was diametrically different from Khosrow's, showcasing the rich diversity of human personalities. Naser was impulsive, exuberant, plain-spoken, and forthright. In contrast, Khosrow had a laid-back temperament and would assert himself after considering all aspects. He would make difficult decisions without having the spotlight on him, which seldom attracted the guards.

One day, Naser's honesty got him into trouble. Along with three others, he was accused of incitement and sentenced to thirty lashes in front of us. After a week in isolation, the four were brought to our ward for punishment. Their shirts were removed, and they were forced to lie face down on a bench. It was extremely traumatic to witness this brutal event, especially because it involved one of my best friends. After this cruel ordeal, they were taken back to solitary confinement.

For days, I couldn't take my mind off Naser, his wounds, and how long it would take him to heal. Were they going to have a nurse treat his injuries or not? How was he coping with the pain? What would I have done in his place?

When Naser finally emerged from isolation a few months later, it was a moment of both relief and concern. I refrained from asking about his wounds, mindful of his pride.

"I've been doing a lot of thinking about my encounter with the guards," Naser shared, his eyes reflecting his deep introspection and resilience.

"I've been grappling with it too," I confessed.

"I should have avoided their wrath," he murmured sadly. "Surviving is a difficult balancing act. Showing timid behaviour would suggest that their heavy-handedness pays off. On the other hand, acting too boldly would bring their harshest rage. Consequently, one must constantly consider one's next move to find the right balance."

I nodded in agreement with him and said, "Now that you mention it, I've reached the same conclusion but kept it to myself. With the brutality we face, I imagine others have also found this strategy helpful."

"I've learned now that it's critical to find the right balance every time," he said. "Making a mistake is too costly."

Later, I concluded that this uninterrupted thinking of survival is another torture that could only be quieted during sleep. Our friendship deepened. I enjoyed his company for about the same length of time as that of Khosrow until Naser too entered a never-ending sunset.

Months came and went. As we tried to maintain normality, the authorities periodically disrupted our routines to increase physical and psychological pressure. Regardless, we did our best to continue with many activities, especially our network of classes.

Since I had only completed grade six in Iran, I wanted to improve my Farsi handwriting. I asked another friend, Jahangir, to give me private lessons. He was a lawyer from the province of Azerbaijan, a thin man in his early thirties. In just a few months, he improved my handwriting so much that my wife and parents couldn't believe how substantially my letters had changed. Our sessions lasted for half an hour every day for two months. He would give me practice notes to reproduce and then correct them.

As our lessons continued, I got to know Jahangir on a deeper level, strengthening our friendship. His dedication to fairness and equity, which was beyond reproach, was something I particularly admired. He became another close friend throughout my time in Ward Six, his character earning my utmost respect.

Our first encounter was when we were both being assessed during our stay in the north wing of the first floor. I was impressed by his steadfastness and his refusal to compromise his principles. I left that room a few days earlier than he did and was very happy to see him later in Ward Six.

His temperament was closer to Naser's but more reserved. He was assertive concerning his conviction but less bold on inconsequential affairs.

One incident involving him affected me greatly. We walked into one of the rooms and noticed that a few people were entertaining others with ethnic jokes. The one he heard was about the region of Iranian Azerbaijan. His devotion to self-respect and even-handedness was exceptional.

"Have you forgotten why we are here?" he asked everyone without hesitation. "If people like us don't challenge unfair norms and mores, who will?" He was shouting now.

Silence filled the room as people stared at each other, some with remorse. A person standing close to Jahangir broke the silence: "You are right! It's wrong, I agree."

After a few seconds, while the silence continued, Jahangir and I left the room.

"Your courage is truly inspiring," I whispered.

"I'm sick and tired of one ethnicity belittling another to get a cheap laugh. When are we going to change?" he cried out angrily, his frustration evident.

"Don't you think there's a deeper reason behind this issue?" I asked.

"Yes, there is! Unfortunately, dominant ethnic groups in a region can exert their power through various means. Making antagonistic jokes are a very effective and sinister way for them to wield their power. The sad part is that many people participating in this power play aren't aware of its roots and the harm it causes," he explained, his tone reflecting both his disgust and deep understanding of the issue.

After this incident, I made a promise to myself never to laugh at ethnic jokes that belittle others.

Later, the authorities took Jahangir away and into the abyss.

Unexpectedly, I found that although captivity has many dreadful aspects, it can also have a positive side. I had the pleasure of living in one place with so many who were society's finest. It reminded me of an old Persian saying: *Galleh Kalleh Kardeh* (The herd made an about-face). When a drove of domestic sheep grazes in the wild, the more robust rams, with their magnificent horns, march in front of the herd, and the healthy ewes proceed proudly shoulder to shoulder with their male counterparts. At the tail end are the feeble and frail – the less principled. The herd makes an about-face when a wolf pack attacks from the front. Then, by default, the weak assume the lead, and the strong are the first killed.

During my two years in Ward Six, both the secular and nonsecular individuals lived alongside each other and generally co-operated. Most of us were part of one group or the other and typically acted together, while at other times, we operated separately. For instance, we all refrained from wearing prison clothes, willingly participated in managing the maintenance of the ward, contributed to the network of classes, and didn't work in workshops. On the other hand, while we didn't adhere to the customary religious practices, the non-secular group actively carried out rituals such as praying three times a day (although there are a total of five prayers, the second and third, as well as the fourth and fifth, are combined) and fasting for a month.

Ramadan was the only time this situation posed some difficulty for the secular inmates. Throughout this month, the authorities couldn't force us to fast. So, they pretended we were sick, and since the ill were exempt from fasting, we received food prepared for the infirmary. The quality of the regular meals wasn't much better than the food for the sick; however, the infirmary's food was less palatable due to the lack of variety.

Sometimes, the authorities would bring a few known Tavabs to our ward to intimidate us. To protect ourselves, it became customary for us to boycott the Tavabs by not speaking to them, which, unfortunately, was another humiliating burden they endured.

One day in late 1987 or early 1988, our ward was locked out, and our few hours outside were cancelled. The sick were not allowed to go to the infirmary. Later, it was rumoured that a group on behalf of United Nations' Special Rapporteur of the Commission of Human Rights on Iran Reynaldo Galindo Pohl had visited Evin. We later learned from other inmates that the visitors were only given access to wards One and Two and were somehow convinced that other wards didn't exist. If this was correct, it was a shocking oversight that an international organization had been manipulated into overlooking a significant portion of the prison population. I never found out why such a rumour was circulated and why our ward was cut off from the outside.

Less than two years went by from the time of my capture. At times when we had some privileges, we could visit other rooms, take advantage of the yard downstairs, watch TV occasionally, and receive a limited number of books. Then, harsher conditions would follow. The authorities would close each room and remove some or all our privileges. This cycle continued until the early summer of 1988, when, one day, the prison guards rushed into our ward and ordered, "Everyone in their rooms!" Once the last prisoner hurriedly complied, the guards locked all the doors. After five minutes of absolute silence, which felt like an eternity, one at a time, each room opened and closed. We anxiously waited for them to enter our room at any minute. Despite my experience in prison and some familiarity with the authorities' tactics, the uncertainty of their next move always loomed over us.

Four guards stormed in, stripping the room of all the amenities and leaving without explanation. They confiscated everything from books and purchased food to the TV and other similar items – some of these allowances were given, while others were purchased from the prison during better times.

As the hours dragged on, mostly in complete silence, my dread of their impending aggression intensified. I fixed my eyes on the door, my fear of the unknown mounting. With each passing moment, the hope of any announcement dwindled, leaving us distressed. Our need to use the washroom became increasingly urgent, forcing us to use a container in the corner of the room as a urinal. Finally, after more than eight hours had crawled by, the door creaked open.

"You have twenty minutes to go to the washroom. From now until further notice, you'll have two chances to use the washroom, once in the morning and once in the afternoon," one of the guards announced.

After this, we had to organize. With limited resources and many people, the careful management of every aspect of our daily routine became of the utmost importance.

The washroom had three showers, three toilets, and a long sink to wash clothes. We divided ourselves into three sections. The first and second groups were assigned to wash their clothes or use the showers. Two toilets were allocated to the third group, who needed to use them more. The other toilet was for the rest of us, who only needed to urinate. Tasks were to be executed so that everyone finished in twenty minutes. Assuming thirty people were in a room, an average calculation would yield two minutes per individual to use the toilets. If one person took longer than scheduled, he would cause the next person to have less time. Above all, one way or another, everyone needed to use the toilet within the twenty-minute limit. Later, it became evident that this situation had a few side effects for some of us, the most common being hemorrhoids.

As the lockdown continued, I began to think again about the reasons behind the prison management's constant shift between a more relaxed atmosphere and more punitive living conditions. I was more interested in the psychological implications and their motives. There was no doubt that these tactics significantly disturbed the mental state of those who were more susceptible to the harsh conditions and often struggled to cope. Even those better equipped to handle the stress weren't immune to their effects. They likely bore some latent scars without being aware of the ramifications.

After some weeks, conditions became less tense again. The doors opened, and we used the washroom as needed. This situation continued for a few weeks until one night. It was around 10 p.m. or 11 p.m. when the guards rushed in again.

"The prisoners whose names I announce will put their blindfolds on and line up in the hallway," said one of the guards, his voice shattering the silence like a sudden thunderstorm.

As he read from the list, I couldn't help but notice that, with a few exceptions, they were mainly the names of secular inmates. After some minutes, my name was called.

I got up and joined the others. Then, with one guard in front and a few behind, they led us out of the ward toward the lobby of the main floor, and out of the building into the dead of night.

18
The Unknown

The first condition for changing reality is to understand it.
Eduardo Galeano

A sense of anticipation filled the air as we circled the swimming pool, heading toward the west side. We marched south down the hill toward the old buildings, knowing that we were about to enter the hallway of the Old Wards. The guard leading us stopped in front of a large door, unlocked it, and, with a command that echoed through the hallway, said, "Get in!"

Upon entering the ward, my eyes immediately scanned the hallway, eager to take in the sight of the other occupants. After being assigned a room, it became clear that the people previously in our new ward had recently arrived from Gohardasht Prison. I also noticed that only prisoners from Ward Six – the fourth floor of the building up on the hill – were moved to where we just arrived. Apart from some exceptions, we were all secular prisoners. This two-storey edifice, Band-a Ghadeem, was comprised of several wards (maybe five, six, or seven) side by side, abutting each other as well as the rear wall of the administration building. Each ward was a rectangular space comprised of an L-shaped building and a yard, which faced the back wall of the next ward. A hallway connected all the units to the administration building.

In the late summer of 1988, I was in one of the Band-a Ghadeem wards when a few inmates discovered through Morse code with other wards that something horrendous was happening: numerous people were being executed. The news struck me like a thunderbolt, shattering the thin veil of hope that things might change for the better. The details surrounding the executions were unclear. A stream of vague messages came in from Gohardasht and other parts of Evin, making it difficult to comprehend the unfolding events, especially since we were already sentenced. Why would they resort to such drastic measures? Many of us were in disbelief, struggling to accept the reasoning behind it. But as more information circulated, I became convinced that something serious was occurring.

We discovered that people were being tried before a second court – *dadgah-h vigeh* (unique court or death commission). Later, we learned that the secular and non-secular inmates were asked different questions. The former were asked if they believed in Islam and the latter if they affirmed allegiance to the Islamic Republic of Iran. The word "why" swam in my mind. Why did the authorities decide to go to such extremes? Most people around me were non-violent individuals whose only "crime" was to hope for a different world.

As the atmosphere became increasingly horrid, a flood of thoughts overwhelmed me. Was I underestimating the gravity of the news? Do we seek comfort in unrealistic optimism during difficult circumstances? For a moment, I was lost in a whirlwind, struggling to distinguish reality from fiction. In these existential moments, it's paradoxical that the need for introspection amidst the multitude sparks a longing for solitude, while at the same time, there's a yearning for the security of others' company.

All of us in Band-a Ghadeem were to face a second trial. And so, nearly everyone felt compelled to gather their thoughts and come up with an appropriate statement to present to the "court." Some believed that mentioning Article 23 of the Constitution of the Islamic Republic of Iran, relating to civil society's freedom of thought, was a good defence. It states that "the investigation of individuals' beliefs is forbidden."

Others were convinced this was simply a statement on paper and that the authorities would easily bypass the constitution without any reservation. They pointed to numerous examples of other countries that had conveniently ignored their constitutions and the spirit of their laws. Ultimately, it was a decision that each person had to make in their "fortress of solitude."

Ironically, no one knew of the unique court's position: delivering the "ultimate verdict" – we were unaware that our lives depended mainly on our response during this second trial. We were at the authorities' disposal and had no idea that we were about to become victims of a mass execution scheme.

After careful consideration, I concluded that my best course of action was to stick to the same narrative I had consistently presented: my life story. Throughout numerous interrogations, I had continually maintained that my acquaintance with the Iranian culture and religion was limited.

The atmosphere was tense. We were all waiting for something to happen but didn't know when or what. Most were silent and in deep thought. Here and there, some were whispering. Eyes told a lot. Looking around, I saw people's gazes fixed on one spot without seeing. Other eyes were screaming a silent message. These scenes reminded me of my previous interrogations. Strangely, I thought of the advantage of being blindfolded; uncovered, one's eyes can tell their own story. It's ironic: interrogators want information, yet they are so afraid of being exposed that they unwittingly hamper their purpose. Supposedly shrewd people sometimes miss important considerations due to desires like power and intimidation.

I waited for my turn, knowing that something terrible was to come. Just a day before, an older man, allegedly a member of the central committee of a political group, had been summoned. I had come to know this amiable-looking, white-haired man whose face bore the weight of the intense anguish he had endured over the past few years. The guard shouted, "All your belongings!" He was the first person called and was treated separately from the rest of the ward. As he made his way up the steps, glancing back, his gaze met mine. We both knew that these were his final hours. In that silent exchange, we bid our farewells, my heart heavy with the knowledge of his profound suffering.

A bearded man with a pot-belly opened the door of the ward. His longer-than-usual rumpled shirt hung over his pants – customary for government supporters – and the backs of his shoes folded under his heels, making them into slippers. Was he bearing the much-anticipated news? He looked around and suddenly yelled out a name. I was surprised not to hear mine. A temporary feeling of relief came over me, quickly overshadowed by guilt. Both feelings at once. Is it natural to feel solace at the expense of others? I had no answer, yet I couldn't help feeling less anxious. The bearded man left with his prey, and a few minutes passed; he returned and took one more from among us. This process continued for an hour until I heard my name.

Before leaving the ward, he said, "Put your blindfold on!" I hesitated, my mind blank with confusion. What was waiting for me outside the ward?

Walking alongside the guard, I recalled receiving my first sentence. The "court personnel" called me into a room.

"Don't think that because you haven't been in this country for some time, we will send you to one of those bogus and pretentious courts with a fancy lawyer as they have in the West. Herewith, you are sentenced to three years," he shouted.

As I looked at the guard's folded shoes, visible below the bottom of my blindfold, I mused that about a year was left of my three years.

What will they do with me? Will I see the end of my sentence? But who knows, maybe I'm overthinking it. It's too far away … among those thoughts, the weight of uncertainty loomed larger than all the others..

Following the guard down a dimly lit corridor toward an unknown place, my apprehension began to build. The air was thick with a musty smell, and the sound of our footsteps echoed off the cold concrete walls. Time slowed; I peeked down to navigate. I noticed the guard was distracted momentarily, allowing me to look around. I had heard that this building in the southern part of Evin Prison was one of the first structures built during the Shah's regime.

As I continued surveying my surroundings, the tired look of the building, worn down by the weight of its history, captured my attention. The walls, marked with the passage of time, bore witness to the many stories that had unfolded within.

What if each mark could tell its story of what happened here in the years past? I thought.

The building emanated an eerie feeling with its age and the unknown circumstances facing me. The abundance of concrete, now devoid of its original colour, seemed to epitomize gloom, conveying a premonition of imminent danger.

We reached the end of a hallway and paused near a door. From under the bottom of my blindfold, I noticed a long line to my right. Scores of people were sitting on the floor, blindfolded, with their backs against the wall. To my left, a few men were seated in the same way. I recognized some from both lines as people who had been called before me.

After some minutes, the door opened. While adjusting his blindfold, an inmate was ushered out and to the extremely long line.

"Go in and remove your blindfold." The guard's voice pierced the silence, his command sudden and jarring.

As I stepped into the room, I spotted the man I knew all too well – the supervisor of the wards on the hill. Memories of his relentless interrogations and our sleepless night came rushing back, but I remained composed. "Sit down!" the same man shouted, his voice adding to the intense pressure I was feeling.

I sat facing an *akhond* (clergy, or so-called judge), with the supervisor standing behind me. Two or three people – I can't remember exactly – were seated at a long table to my right, later revealed to be the "prosecutors."

As soon as I sat down, the "judge" asked me, "Do you believe in Islam?"

I replied that I had left Iran at the age of twelve and was not familiar with Islam, a response that seemed to test his patience.

"Did you live with your family?" asked the judge, his voice showing his anger.

I answered no, stating that I lived with an American family.

One of the prosecutors, a man with a stern expression, loudly asked, "Were there any Iranians around that could inform you about the teachings of Islam?"

I replied, "No."

This only seemed to enrage him further, and he demanded, "Do you know the pillars of Islam?"

Again, I responded, "No."

"Do you know what *Ma'ad* is?" he pressed on.

"No."

Later, I learned it was one of the pillars of Islam. At that moment, I noticed the judge glancing at the person behind me. His gaze appeared to indicate some non-verbal communication – perhaps the judge wanted to verify my statement with the guard's records.

"Put him in solitary confinement," the judge declared. "He will remain there until he learns the teachings of Islam." His words hit me like a bolt of lightning.

I had no idea his statement was a signal, a code for placing me in the shorter line. I looked the judge in the eye, my mind reeling with confusion, and said, "I can't learn about Islam in these conditions."

He became livid and screamed, "Take him away."

The person behind me grabbed my arm and said, "Put your blindfold on!" He led me out of the room to the shorter line and told me to sit down.

We waited there for a few hours before being moved to a small room. Upon entering and removing my blindfold, I noticed fewer than a dozen people. I was held there for another four or five hours until someone came in and escorted me to the "Tranquility Ward."

19
The Last Walk

Men are never really willing to die except for the sake of freedom: therefore, they do not believe in dying completely.
Albert Camus

I entered a cell that resembled one I had been in a few years before. The first day was bearable. I felt less distressed, a drastic contrast to the agony of the previous few months. However, after a day, I had a vague suspicion that this time would be different. There was a lingering unease, a feeling that perhaps an extended stay awaited me.

As I sat in that cell, I thought of people's capacity for resilience in the face of unbearable tragedy. If our will to live is the most critical drive, why do some of us choose death?

The irony struck me. Those of us who want less suffering for others often endure the harshest punishments. We're labelled as agitators, and our intentions are distorted. Yet, our resolve is constantly tested, tempting us to give in, in return for which, we are promised a better life. Some succumb and bend the knee. Others stand tall and try to make a difference.

It was a chilling revelation; while in this cell, I had no idea that everyone in the long line and many non-secular prisoners tried elsewhere in Evin were executed.

The sheer scale of the executions was a shock I could hardly comprehend. I came to understand that the authorities' infamous justification for the mass executions of the secular prisoners was rooted in their interpretation of two types of an apostate, someone who has renounced religion: one was *mortad-e fetri* (intrinsic apostate); the other was *mortad-e milli* (national apostate). According to them, the former was someone born into a Muslim family who turned away from Islam after puberty. Their punishment was the death penalty. In their view, the latter was someone born into a Muslim family who had been away from an Islamic environment before puberty, and during the years of separation, no attempts were made to familiarize them with Islamic thinking. The sentence for this type of apostate was something other than the death penalty. After some time, it became clear to me that I had escaped execution because, according to their definition, the judge had labelled me a "national apostate," possibly due to my departure from Iran at a young age – before puberty – and my living with American families.

When I first heard about the tragic deaths, recurring thoughts haunted me: *How can I go on knowing that my best friends and thousands of others went to the gallows? Will I be mentally fully or partially alive? Will there be a day that their memory doesn't haunt me, or will it always stay with me?*

During and after the executions, the authorities used various schemes to divert the domestic and international publics' attention from the mass killings. Many prisoners who didn't face a second trial were granted amnesty, but the authorities attempted to make it seem like all prisoners were pardoned. They even staged a ceremony in the centre of Tehran, parading a few recently released prisoners to give the appearance of a widespread amnesty.

This mass killing was a watershed moment in Iranian history. At a certain point, the authorities were forced to end the war with Iraq and turn a new page – on 17 July 1988, Iran accepted a UN-brokered ceasefire. Shortly after, an Iranian militant group supported by the Iraqi Army based in Iraq seized the opening and attacked the Kurdistan province. Most Iranians were surprised and not supportive of this attack. However, following the militant group's defeat, the Iranian authorities may have used this event to address once and for all their long-standing issue of how to deal with the problem of political prisoners.

In other words, as part of their goal, they aimed to semi-indiscriminately eliminate as many political prisoners as possible, even those who were not involved in the attack. However, the fate of the leadership of different groups was not indiscriminately decided. They might have thought that in the chaos of that period, their mass killings would stay under the radar of the general public and the world. Therefore, to justify their actions to their base of support, they strategically attached a religious rationale to a political decision. They also believed it would help President Akbar Hashemi Rafsanjani's quest to attract foreign investments by mitigating the human rights issue, with the question of political prisoners as its central point. To this end, they released numerous prisoners and were ready to showcase a limited number of those still incarcerated to both domestic and international audiences, thereby demonstrating their commitment to "human rights."

My belief in their semi-indiscriminate elimination was reinforced when I heard of the execution of Ahmad, a boy I knew from Ward Six. He was an eighteen-year-old who had no political experience. During one of our conversations, he voluntarily told me the details of his capture. He explained that his supposed crime was to affix a flyer on the window of a telephone booth. Little distinction was made between a higher- and a lower-level political prisoner. All suffered the same fate.

They suspended all our visitations and letters for about four months before and after I arrived in solitary confinement. We were completely isolated from the outside. As I entered a life of isolation again, I had to adjust quickly, even though I had gained much experience. I learned there is a significant difference between feeling lonely and being alone. The challenge is overcoming the former and getting to know the latter.

Following a long period of isolation, the cell door opened one afternoon, and someone said, "Put your blindfold on and come out."

After a labyrinth of stairways and a hallway, I was taken outside and eventually to one of the wards in the Band-a Ghadeem, which was less than a third full. It looked identical to the wards I had lived in before. Others there were either from the shorter line during the second trial or had arrived from various prisons. Each had a different reason for being alive. There, I heard the most shocking news – conservatively, more than 2,800[1] prisoners had been killed within three to four months, mainly in Evin and Gohardasht prisons.

I realized that my closest friends – Khosrow, Naser, Jahangir, and others – were all executed.

I felt like part of me had gone with them. *How was I going to endure such agony? After this tragedy, can one live a "normal" life? If I came out of this ordeal alive, would I carry their memory for the rest of my life?* I entered the ward and walked around awhile, their absence evoking a morbid feeling. Everything seemed out of place. It's strange – in extraordinary times, the same surroundings appear different. It felt as if I had entered an unrecognizable time and place.

Tales of how the unsuspecting prisoners went to the gallows were passed around. The most agreed-upon account was that they were hanged in the auditorium. It was rumoured that they only became aware of their fate in the last queue. Many nights, I had nightmares. I imagined being in line waiting for execution. I could hear the thud of people falling around me. The sound of them gasping for air was unbearable.

Although my life's history was an aberration compared to most others in prison, I asked myself why such a trivial factor should be so life-altering. In certain periods of our lives, the direction in which we find ourselves is determined so randomly that the whole situation becomes absurd. The arbitrariness of my being alive became a source of intense guilt.

After a few weeks, we were all summoned for an interrogation, a stark departure from the usual one-on-one grilling. Blindfolded, we formed a line in the hallway. A guard would guide each of us to a chair before the interrogator. After the questioning, we were directed to either the right or left side of the hallway. My turn came after about five minutes, the guard's voice echoing as the prisoner in front of me vacated the chair.

"Sit down!" I sat. "I'm aware that all of you know what happened to the other prisoners. If you don't want the same outcome for yourself, you need to give a video interview showing your remorse," the inquisitor said.

A few seconds passed, then I replied, "I can't."

"Take him away!" he shouted.

I got up and walked toward the line to my right.

After this ordeal was over, someone came to my side of the hallway and yelled, "All of you get up and follow me."

Slightly more than a handful of us returned to our previous ward to face the most challenging twelve hours of our lives. We all awaited the verdict, constantly imagining what would happen; it was a terrifying experience. The emotional struggle was overwhelming, with a feeling of numbness overshadowing all other senses. The thought that consumed me the most was my son's future without me. He was vulnerable and needed my attention; the idea of him growing up without a father for the rest of his life was chilling. I no longer felt anxious for the door to open; I pushed aside trivial thoughts and drew strength from remembering the past.

How should one react when the end is near? What can one discuss in such circumstances? Nightfall arrived, and still, nothing happened. A dreadful silence enveloped the entire block. I felt as if I were witnessing an enormous cloud forming an eerie, dark shadow just before the approach of a vicious storm.

Later that night, the door burst open, and the guards rushed in. Their sudden appearance and abrupt entrance, like a bolt from the blue, interrupted our thoughts. One of them read out three names, including mine.

"Follow me with all your belongings," he said, his casual tone a stark contrast to the moment's gravity, a tension that hung in the air like a heavy fog.

Blindfolded, we walked behind him in a single line. A gentle breeze brushed my face as we stepped outside the building. I could feel the freshness of the air more than ever. The sharp tweeting sound of a bird reminded me of nature's presence and reassured me that life would continue with or without me.

Where was he leading us? We followed him up the hill and into a building, our destination shrouded in mystery.

He stopped before a solitary cell and yelled, "Get in!"

Is this a temporary holding place? How can three people stay in such a small area? After a few hours, I had mixed feelings. In a way, having all of us in a space designed for a single person was challenging, especially when one of us needed to use the toilet. On the other hand, not being alone was comforting. Still, regular conversations and occasional smiles felt strange after the mass executions. As time passed, the other two were taken away; I never saw them again.

In the corner of my cell, sitting on an army blanket, my back to the wall and thighs to my chest, I thought of the brutality of the past few years. I became convinced that when most political prisoners are ridiculed, humiliated, and suffer hardship, they usually find any means to regain their dignity. So, unintentionally, the authorities create hard-core dissidents out of many who might have just been simple activists.

It was the spring of 1989, less than three years had passed since my capture. I wasn't sure how many inmates from Ward Six were still alive. Having been in solitary confinement many times before, I vividly remembered my last stay in the same building, especially when I stepped out to end my isolation. I remembered how intensely my senses were awakened, and how the feelings of resilience and fatigue nibbled at each other.

This time round, I was more doubtful about the circumstances. However, I had learned from my experiences in solitary confinement that the only way to survive and maintain sanity was to have an unwavering state of mind and purpose. I had witnessed occasions when people unprepared for the "Tranquility Ward" completely broke down and lost their sanity, shouting and banging on their cell doors until the prison guards intervened, beating them, and then taking them away.

To endure solitude, I knew I had to mentally prepare myself for a more extended stay than I might have anticipated. This meant keeping my expectations in check. If, by any chance, I came out earlier than expected, I would have gained an additional advantage in my psychological struggle for survival.

After some weeks, an interrogator called me. This time, he didn't mention a video interview. Instead, he placed a piece of paper in front of me, his hands steady, his eyes unwavering, intensifying the uncertainty of my situation.

"Signing this is your only chance for freedom."

Even though I was skeptical about the veracity of his claim, I wanted to believe that there might be some truth in what he said. I was sitting in a chair with a small table attached to its side. After placing the paper on the table, he left the room. It was half the size of a regular sheet of paper with two handwritten lines on it. I read it multiple times. They wanted me to express my repugnance toward a secular guerrilla group that had carried out armed resistance against the Shah's regime.

They must have known that after the revolution, a significant faction from that group had abandoned their strategy of armed struggle and dropped the guerrilla part from their name. I was surprised: why did they choose this group? Except for self-defence, I'm against violence. For a moment, I felt lucky. Perhaps they had mistakenly written this short paragraph. On the other hand, was there a deliberate attempt to associate me with this group? An inner voice objected: *You have never believed in violence; theoretically, signing it can't make a difference*. But then another voice would say, *Delve deeper into your conscience. Is it right to sign something that's been coerced?* As I grappled with these thoughts, a short time felt like an eternity. The stress was so intense that my mind was in a whirlwind. The battle between love and self-preservation, instinct and rationality, was fierce. As famously said, we rationalize our actions after our instinctual reaction.

Once again, my persistent inner voice bombarded me with questions. Would all the suffering I had endured during these three years be rendered pointless by signing this piece of paper? What if I signed and found out that freedom was just an illusion? By refusing to sign, would I be demonstrating my strength of character or capitulating to absurdity? When faced with unreasonable and brutal people, does signing become a form of justification? Would I be standing on my principles or retreating into irrationality? Were they outmanoeuvring me, or was I witnessing confused people claiming to be crafty? Perhaps it's neither of the two.

In extreme situations where whatever one does, the outcome is undesirable, a toll, whether physical or psychological, must ultimately be paid. My feelings were mixed. Should I entertain a sense of guilt or recognize the irrationality of the moment? It was one of the most critical moments of my life. Throughout my imprisonment, I resisted this type of request. A voice would say, *For the most part, you are against violence.* The other voice would say, *You are rationalizing your situation.* These conflicting thoughts were eating away at me.

Many episodes came to mind, marking the moment's gravity for signing or not signing. I remembered a turning point when it was announced that Ayatollah Montazeri – second-in-command to Ayatollah Khomeini – had criticized the mass killings and was rapidly falling out of favour with Ayatollah Khomeini. At that moment, I became convinced that the emergence of one faction to the detriment of another within the government had already spilled over to the prisons, creating much harsher conditions.

All along, my refusal to give a TV interview or sign a letter of remorse, at least in my mind, had an existential consequence. They had tried many tactics to no avail, including pressuring my wife to come to Evin and convince me to give an interview.

"It's up to him to make the final decision," she told them.

It's not easy to re-evaluate a stance that one has strongly held with great conviction for some time. Where should I draw the line? I knew that participating in an interview was out of the question. I was also concerned with the future impact of my decision – if there was a future. Would they gain an advantage by my signing? Was I walking into a trap? Ultimately, I reasoned that the document didn't mention remorse, only about rejecting a group I disagreed with. Then I thought, even if my logic had elements of rationalization, I had to decide.

Regardless of their next move, I signed, knowing that this was my line in the sand for a faint chance of freedom.

After this episode, I was taken back to my cell. During this time, my dreams became very active. One night, I would dream of freedom; another night, of being executed. A recurring dream was hearing others being put to death while I waited in line for the same fate. In some dreams, I wondered if my unconscious mind was acting partly as a defence mechanism. Even more, while awake, I thought of the executions. How did those inmates react while waiting? What would I have done?

Several days had passed when a guard, his face breaking into a hopeful smile, delivered unexpected news: a chance for freedom. Was this a cruel game they were playing to torment me or were they telling the truth? The next day, the guard returned and unlocked the door.

"Get ready! I'll come back in an hour."

I packed up whatever I had and got ready. An hour and a half came and went. Nothing happened. I had enough experience to avoid falling into their trap. As soon as I was sure nothing would come of it, I unpacked my belongings and placed them precisely like before. I knew that continued anticipation was the worst mental state to fall into, and the best remedy was to erase it from the mind completely.

Am I awake or lost in one of my daydreams after a short nap? The solitary confinement door, a symbol of oppression, creaks open, and a guard shouts, "All your belongings!" I hastily gather my things, am blindfolded, and follow the man. I anticipate this walk to be my final steps in Evin, a ritual I have lived repeatedly in my dreams. But as we descend the hill, I suddenly become uncertain of the guard's intention and direction. Alarm grips me with such intensity that I think of those dearest to my heart who faced that exact suspicion on a dreadful day some months ago and then were plunged into the abyss. Where precisely in their last walk had that feeling come to them? At the moment, my heart ached, and I felt their same fear. Mine proved to be momentary; theirs was a relentless, consuming terror.

Acknowledgments

I want to express my heartfelt gratitude to my family for their unwavering support and encouragement. I also thank Connie Dilley for being the first to read my original manuscript and for her insightful suggestions.

I am deeply grateful to my editors, Lynn Cunningham, Amanda Lewis, and Lisa Thomas-Tench, for their generous support, understanding, and professionalism. Additionally, I want to acknowledge my indexer, Alexandra Peace, for her hard work.

I would like to extend my appreciation to the exceptional team at McGill-Queen's University Press (MQUP), particularly senior editor Emily Andrew. Her guidance and expertise enhanced the quality of my manuscript, leading to its approval. Emily's excellent communication with my three anonymous readers provided invaluable feedback and constructive critiques that significantly improved my work.

Equally, I want to express my profound gratitude to the staff of MQUP, including the design and marketing teams, for their support throughout the publishing process. A special thank you goes to managing editor Kathleen Fraser for her timely advice and assistance. Lastly, I am incredibly thankful to MQUP's copy editor, Eleanor Gasparik, whose diligence, knowledge, and meticulous attention to detail helped transform my manuscript into a polished book.

Notes

PROLOGUE

1 Ervand Abrahamian, *Tortured Confessions: Prisons and Public Recantations in Modern Iran* (University of California Press, 1999), 105, 135.

CHAPTER FIVE

1 Chicki Mallan, *Catalina Island Handbook* (Moon Publications, 1992), 3.

2 Howard Means, *67 Shots: Kent State and the End of American Innocence* (Da Capo Press, 2016), 141, 147, 159.

CHAPTER SIX

1 Ali Rahnema, *The Political History of Modern Iran: Revolution, Reaction and Transformation, 1905 to the Present* (I.B. Tauris, Bloomsbury Publishing, 2023), 352.

2 Abbas Amanat, *Iran: A Modern History* (Yale University Press, 2017), 706–7.

CHAPTER SEVEN

1 Abbas Amanat, *Iran: A Modern History* (Yale University Press, 2017), 737.

2 Ervand Abrahamian, *A History of Modern Iran* (Cambridge University Press, 2008), xxi.

1 Ibid., 118–22.

CHAPTER FIFTEEN

1 Ervand Abrahamian, *The Iranian Mojahedin* (I.B. Tauris, Yale University Press, 1989), 38.

CHAPTER NINETEEN

1 Ervand Abrahamian, *A History of Modern Iran* (Cambridge University Press, 2008), 181.

Index

Footprints Series
Jane Errington, Editor

1 *Blatant Injustice*
The Story of a Jewish Refugee from Nazi Germany Imprisoned in Britain and Canada during World War II
Walter W. Igersheimer
Edited and with a foreword by Ian Darragh

2 *Against the Current*
Memoirs
Boris Ragula

3 *Margaret Macdonald*
Imperial Daughter
Susan Mann

4 *My Life at the Bar and Beyond*
Alex K. Paterson

5 *Red Travellers*
Jeanne Corbin and Her Comrades
Andrée Lévesque

6 *The Teeth of Time*
Remembering Pierre Elliott Trudeau
Ramsay Cook

7 *The Greater Glory*
Thirty-seven Years with the Jesuits
Stephen Casey

8 *Doctor to the North*
Thirty Years Treating Heart Disease among the Inuit
John H. Burgess

9 *Dal and Rice*
Wendy M. Davis

10 *In the Eye of the Wind*
A Travel Memoir of Prewar Japan
Ron Baenninger and Martin Baenninger

11 *I'm from Bouctouche, Me*
Roots Matter
Donald J. Savoie

12 *Alice Street*
A Memoir
Richard Valeriote

13 *Crises and Compassion*
From Russia to the Golden Gate
John M. Letiche

14 *In the Eye of the China Storm*
A Life Between East and West
Paul T.K. Lin with Eileen Chen Lin

15 *Georges and Pauline Vanier*
Portrait of a Couple
Mary Frances Coady

16 *Blitzkrieg and Jitterbugs*
College Life in Wartime, 1939–1942
Elizabeth Hillman Waterston

17 *Harrison McCain*
Single-Minded Purpose
Donald J. Savoie

18 *Discovering Confederation*
A Canadian's Story
Janet Ajzenstat

19 *Expect Miracles*
Recollections of a Lucky Life
David M. Culver with Alan Freeman

20 *Building Bridges*
Victor C. Goldbloom

21 *Call Me Giambattista*
A Personal and Political Journey
John Ciaccia

22 *Smitten by Giraffe*
My Life as a Citizen Scientist
Anne Innis Dagg

23 *The Oil Has Not Run Dry*
The Story of My Theological Pathway
Gregory Baum

24 *My Peerless Story*
It Starts with the Collar
Alvin Cramer Segal

25 *Wrestling with Life*
From Hungary to Auschwitz to Montreal
George Reinitz with Richard King

26 *Never Rest on Your Ores*
Building a Mining Company, One Stone at a Time
Norman B. Keevil

27 *The Making of a Museum*
Judith Nasby

28 *Gold's Rounds*
Medicine, McGill, and Growing Up Jewish in Montreal
Phil Gold

29 *Ghost Stories*
On Writing Biography
Judith Adamson

30 *What Ukrainian Elections Taught Me about Democracy*
Jane Cooper

31 *The Darkest Night Brings Longer Days*
Surviving War and Iran's Evin Prison
Sirous Houshmand